Cryptocurrency Trading

The Art of Cryptocurrency Trading:

Strategies for Profiting

in the Digital Asset Market

Ethan Harrington

TABLE OF CONTENTS

INTRODUCTION

Cryptocurrency trading has emerged as a profitable and exciting opportunity in the world of finance. A growing number of individuals from all walks of life are entering the cryptocurrency trading market to take advantage of the enormous potential that digital assets and blockchain technology provide. But navigating the intricate and unpredictable digital asset market involves more than simply good fortune; it also calls for a thorough comprehension of the strategies and techniques that can result in winning trades.

We will delve into the fascinating world of cryptocurrency trading in this e-book, "Cryptocurrency Trading: The Art of Cryptocurrency Trading - Strategies for Profiting in the Digital Asset Market," and we'll give you the knowledge and abilities you need to navigate this dynamic environment confidently.

We'll start by laying a strong basis for cryptocurrency trading by defining it and highlighting the advantages and risks of this type of investment. Understanding the cryptocurrency industry is crucial, thus we will look at the fundamentals of cryptocurrencies, significant participants, market trends, and factors affecting cryptocurrency prices.

Although it may seem daunting to begin trading cryptocurrencies, we will walk you through the process. You will learn helpful information to assist you as you start your trading career, from creating a cryptocurrency wallet to picking a trustworthy exchange and comprehending various cryptocurrency orders.

For trading decisions, a strong grasp of both fundamental and technical analysis is essential. We'll go over how to examine a project's fundamentals, gauge market acceptance, and keep abreast of news and events that could affect cryptocurrency pricing. We will also cover technical analysis, giving you the knowledge and skills to examine price charts, identify patterns, and use a variety of indicators to make data-driven trading decisions.

The secret to success in the cryptocurrency market is creating efficient trading techniques. We'll look at both short- and long-term techniques, dive into day-, swing-, and position-trading techniques, and emphasize the value of risk management and emotional restraint when trading.

We will introduce you to advanced trading strategies including margin trading, arbitrage strategies, algorithmic trading, and social trading as your knowledge and expertise progress. You can increase your trading performance and profitability with the aid of these strategies.

It's vital to assess and choose the best cryptocurrencies for your portfolio. We will assist you in learning how to explore and assess cryptocurrencies, evaluate tokenomics and utility, comprehend whitepapers and roadmaps, and identify intriguing investment prospects.

However, it is significant to mention that trading cryptocurrencies entail risks. We will discuss these risks, provide a warning, and highlight the significance of following the law and getting competent guidance. We'll also talk about how trading cryptocurrencies may have implications for taxes.

Staying informed and adjusting to market dynamics are essential to succeed in the constantly evolving cryptocurrency market. Reliable news sources, cryptocurrency communities, and techniques for monitoring market sentiment will all be covered. We will also stress the value of ongoing education and skill improvement in order to stay competitive in this quick-paced sector.

By the time you finish reading this e-book, you'll have a thorough understanding of cryptocurrency trading, improved your analytical abilities, and developed effective strategies for navigating the market for digital assets. This e-book will be your essential guide to making money in the fascinating world of cryptocurrency trading, whether you are a beginner trader or an experienced investor wishing to broaden your horizons. So let's embark on this adventure together and discover the secrets of trading cryptocurrencies.

CHAPTER

I

Understanding the
Cryptocurrency Market

Basics of Cryptocurrencies

Cryptocurrencies have revolutionized the financial landscape, offering a decentralized and secure means of conducting transactions and storing value. As digital currencies powered by blockchain technology, they have garnered immense attention and popularity in recent years. In this section, we will delve into the basics of cryptocurrencies, exploring their definition, underlying technology, and key characteristics that distinguish them from traditional forms of currency.

Cryptocurrencies, often called digital or virtual currencies, are digital assets designed to serve as mediums of exchange. They employ cryptographic techniques to secure transactions and control the creation of new units. Cryptocurrencies can be traced back to 2009 when the enigmatic figure, Satoshi Nakamoto, introduced Bitcoin, the first and most well-known cryptocurrency.

Blockchain technology, a decentralized and transparent ledger system, is at the heart of cryptocurrencies. A distributed network of computers, or nodes, known as a blockchain is used to maintain and validate transactions. Each transaction is grouped into a "block" and added to a chain of existing blocks, forming an immutable record. This technology ensures transparency, security, and resistance to fraud.

One of the key characteristics of cryptocurrencies is decentralization. Unlike traditional currencies controlled by central banks or governments, cryptocurrencies operate on decentralized networks. This means that no single entity has complete authority over the currency, fostering a sense of trust and eliminating the need for intermediaries.

Security and anonymity are also crucial aspects of cryptocurrencies. Cryptocurrencies employ cryptographic techniques to secure transactions and control the creation of new units. Public and private keys are used to authenticate and verify ownership, ensuring secure and tamper-resistant transactions. Additionally, while transactions are recorded on the blockchain, participants' identities remain pseudonymous, providing a degree of privacy.

Cryptocurrencies also have a limited supply. Most cryptocurrencies have a finite supply, often determined by predefined algorithms. For instance, the 21 million coin limit on Bitcoin provides scarcity and the possibility of rising value over time.

Moreover, cryptocurrencies offer global accessibility. They transcend borders, enabling seamless and near-instantaneous transactions on a global scale. As long as one has an internet connection, they can participate in the cryptocurrency ecosystem, fostering financial inclusion and cross-border transactions.

Cryptocurrency mining plays a pivotal role in the creation and verification of transactions. Miners, individuals or entities with specialized hardware and software, validate transactions and add them to the blockchain. This process involves solving complex mathematical puzzles, which consumes computational power and energy. Miners are incentivized with newly minted cryptocurrency units and transaction fees.

Bitcoin (BTC) is the pioneer of cryptocurrencies and remains the most widely recognized and dominant digital currency. It paved the way for the development of numerous other cryptocurrencies and continues to hold significant value and market capitalization.

Ethereum (ETH) introduced the concept of smart contracts, which are self-executing agreements with predefined conditions. This functionality has enabled the creation of decentralized applications (dApps) and the issuance of new digital assets through Initial Coin Offerings (ICOs).

Ripple (XRP) aims to revolutionize cross-border payments by facilitating fast and low-cost transactions between financial institutions. It operates on a different consensus mechanism called the Ripple Protocol Consensus Algorithm (RPCA).

Cryptocurrencies have a number of potential advantages. First, they can help the unbanked and underbanked populations worldwide who don't have access to conventional banking institutions become financially included. Second, compared to existing financial systems, cryptocurrency transactions may be more affordable, particularly for international transactions. Finally, decentralized applications and smart contracts created on blockchain platforms enable innovative use cases in a variety of sectors, including supply chain management, identity verification, and decentralized finance.

However, cryptocurrencies also present challenges. Their price volatility is well-known, which can lead to substantial gains or losses for investors. Regulatory uncertainty is another challenge, as governments and regulatory bodies grapple with regulating cryptocurrencies, creating uncertainty and potential legal challenges. Additionally, the scalability of blockchain networks remains a challenge, with concerns about transaction speed and the ability to handle a large number of simultaneous transactions.

Key Players in the Cryptocurrency Market

Since the launch of Bitcoin in 2009, there has been significant growth and development in the cryptocurrency sector. As the popularity of cryptocurrencies soared, numerous key players emerged, contributing to developing and expanding the digital asset ecosystem. In this section, we will explore the key players in the cryptocurrency market, including individuals, companies, and organizations that have played pivotal roles in shaping the industry and driving its progress.

The cryptocurrency revolution began with the introduction of Bitcoin by the mysterious figure known as Satoshi Nakamoto. WWhile Satoshi Nakamoto's exact identity is still a mystery, their groundbreaking whitepaper and the creation of Bitcoin laid the foundation for the entire cryptocurrency market. Nakamoto's vision of a decentralized digital currency continues to inspire and influence the development of new cryptocurrencies.

The first and most recognized cryptocurrency, Bitcoin, has been instrumental in establishing the cryptocurrency industry. It created the foundation for other cryptocurrencies and introduced the idea of blockchain technology. Bitcoin's decentralized nature, limited supply, and secure transactions have garnered significant attention, making it the leading digital asset in market capitalization and mainstream adoption.

Vitalik Buterin, a young programmer and cryptocurrency enthusiast, co-founded Ethereum, a blockchain platform that introduced the concept of smart contracts. Buterin's vision was to create a decentralized platform that enables the development of decentralized applications (DApps) and programmable contracts. Ethereum's innovative approach has fostered a vibrant ecosystem of projects and initiatives, including Initial Coin Offerings (ICOs) and decentralized finance (DeFi) applications.

Binance, founded by Changpeng Zhao (CZ), has emerged as one of the largest and most influential cryptocurrency exchanges globally. Binance has a sizable user base due to its user-friendly interface, broad selection of supported cryptocurrencies, and innovative features. The exchange's native cryptocurrency, Binance Coin (BNB), plays a crucial role in the Binance ecosystem, powering discounted trading fees and other services.

Coinbase, founded by Brian Armstrong, is a prominent cryptocurrency exchange and one of the pioneers in making cryptocurrencies accessible to mainstream users. In order to bridge the gap between conventional finance and the cryptocurrency world, Coinbase provides a user-friendly platform for purchasing, selling, and holding cryptocurrencies. The company's IPO in 2021 further solidified its position as a key player in the cryptocurrency market.

Ripple, co-founded by Chris Larsen and Jed McCaleb, aims to revolutionize cross-border payments and remittances using blockchain technology. Ripple's native cryptocurrency, XRP, plays a central role in facilitating fast and low-cost transactions between financial institutions. The company has partnered with major banks and financial institutions worldwide, positioning itself as a key player in the global financial ecosystem.

Cardano, founded by Charles Hoskinson, is a blockchain platform focusing on security, scalability, and sustainability. With a strong emphasis on academic research and peer-reviewed protocols, Cardano aims to provide a robust foundation for building decentralized applications and enabling secure and scalable transactions. The Cardano blockchain utilizes its native cryptocurrency, ADA, as a means of value transfer within the ecosystem.

Beyond Bitcoin and Ethereum, numerous other influential cryptocurrencies have made their mark in the market. Litecoin, created by Charlie Lee, aims to be a faster and lighter version of Bitcoin, often considered a "silver" to Bitcoin's "gold." Ripple's XRP, mentioned earlier, focuses on facilitating cross-border transactions. Other notable cryptocurrencies include Bitcoin Cash, Chainlink, Polkadot, and many more, each with its unique features and use cases.

Market Analysis and Trends

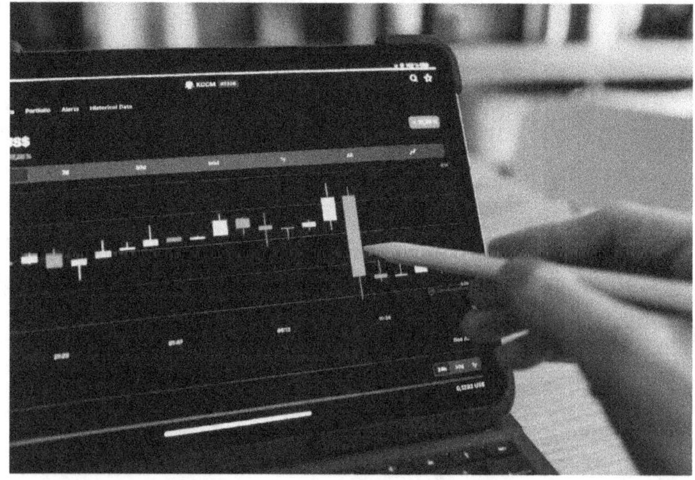

Market analysis and trends play a crucial role in understanding the dynamics and potential opportunities within the cryptocurrency market. It is crucial to keep up with market developments, investor sentiment, and new trends as the digital asset ecosystem develops and grows. In this section, we will explore market analysis and trends in the cryptocurrency market, including the importance of analysis, key indicators, market cycles, and notable trends shaping the industry.

Market analysis is a vital tool for investors and traders in the cryptocurrency market. It involves evaluating various factors to gain insights into the market's current state and potential future movements. Investors can make informed decisions and manage risks by analyzing historical data, trends, and market sentiment. Market analysis provides valuable information for identifying investment opportunities, determining entry and exit points, and devising effective trading strategies.

One of the key indicators used in market analysis is price analysis. This involves examining historical price data to identify patterns, trends, and support/resistance levels. Technical analysis tools such as charts, candlestick patterns, and trend lines are used to interpret price movements and predict future price action.

Trading volume is another crucial indicator. It refers to the total number of assets traded within a specific period. High trading volume often indicates increased market activity and liquidity, suggesting strong interest and participation from investors.

Monitoring trading volume helps gauge market sentiment and identify significant price movements.

Multiplying the price of a cryptocurrency by its circulating supply is used to determine its market capitalization. It estimates a cryptocurrency's overall value and relative size within the market. Analyzing market capitalization helps identify the most prominent cryptocurrencies and assess their market dominance.

Sentiment analysis is another important aspect of market analysis. It involves evaluating market sentiment and investor emotions to gauge market expectations and potential price movements. This analysis can be done through social media monitoring, sentiment indicators, or surveys. Positive sentiment may indicate a bullish market, while negative sentiment may suggest a bearish market.

The cryptocurrency market experiences bullish and bearish trends, driven by various factors, including investor sentiment, technological advancements, regulatory developments, and macroeconomic conditions. Rising prices, increased investor optimism, and a general upward trend characterize bull markets. Bear markets, on the other hand, see declining prices, increased pessimism, and a downward trend. Understanding market cycles helps investors make informed decisions and adjust their strategies accordingly.

The cryptocurrency market is influenced by several notable trends that are shaping its growth and development. One such trend is institutional adoption. Established financial institutions, hedge funds, and corporations increasingly recognize digital assets' potential and invest in cryptocurrencies. This trend brings increased liquidity, stability, and credibility to the market.

Decentralized finance (DeFi) is another significant trend in the cryptocurrency market. The term "DeFi" refers to a group of financial applications created using blockchain technology as decentralized substitutes for established financial institutions. DeFi has gained considerable traction, offering opportunities such as decentralized lending, yield farming, and decentralized exchanges. This trend can reshape conventional financial systems and democratize access to financial services.

Non-fungible tokens (NFTs) have emerged as a vibrant trend in the cryptocurrency market. NFTs are unique digital assets representing ownership or proof of authenticity of a specific item, such as artwork, collectibles, or virtual real estate. The emergence of NFTs highlights the potential of blockchain technology beyond cryptocurrencies, providing new opportunities for artists, creators, and collectors.

Regulatory developments also significantly impact the cryptocurrency market. As the market matures, regulatory frameworks are being developed to address security, fraud, and investor protection concerns. Monitoring regulatory trends is crucial for understanding the legal landscape and its potential impact on the market.

Analyzing market trends involves continuously monitoring and evaluating various factors to identify patterns, anticipate market movements, and make informed investment decisions. By keeping track of market analysis, investors can adjust their strategies, capitalize on emerging trends, and mitigate risks. Knowing market trends also helps identify potential investment opportunities, diversify portfolios, and adapt to changing market conditions.

Factors Influencing Cryptocurrency Prices

The cryptocurrency market is known for its volatility and rapid price fluctuations. Understanding the factors influencing cryptocurrency prices is crucial for investors, traders, and enthusiasts seeking to navigate this dynamic market. In this section, we will explore the various factors that can impact cryptocurrency prices, including supply and demand dynamics, market sentiment, regulatory developments, technological advancements, and macroeconomic factors.

Supply and demand dynamics play a fundamental role in determining cryptocurrency prices. The total supply of a cryptocurrency, often dictated by its underlying protocol or algorithm, can influence its scarcity and perceived value. Cryptocurrencies with limited supplies or decreasing inflation rates may experience upward price pressure due to increased scarcity.

Moreover, the demand for cryptocurrencies can be influenced by several factors. Growing interest from individual and institutional investors, increased adoption in various industries, and recognition by mainstream financial institutions can all contribute to increased demand and potentially drive up prices. Conversely, decreasing demand or negative market sentiment can lead to price declines.

Market sentiment and investor psychology have a significant impact on cryptocurrency prices. Positive sentiment, driven by optimism, technological advancements, or market adoption news, can lead to increased buying activity and upward price movements. Conversely, negative sentiment, fueled by concerns over security breaches, regulatory uncertainty, or negative news events, can trigger selling pressure and price declines.

The cryptocurrency market is known for its high volatility, which can be influenced by investor emotions such as fear, greed, and herd mentality. FUD (Fear, Uncertainty, and Doubt) and FOMO (Fear of Missing Out) can lead to unusual market behavior and inflated price swings. Understanding and analyzing market sentiment is crucial for investors to make informed decisions and manage risks effectively.

Regulatory developments and the legal landscape have a significant impact on cryptocurrency prices. Government regulations, policies, and actions can influence market sentiment and investor confidence. Positive regulatory developments, such as clear guidelines and supportive legislation, can foster trust and legitimacy in cryptocurrencies, potentially leading to price appreciation.

Conversely, regulatory uncertainties or restrictive measures can create uncertainty and negatively impact cryptocurrency prices. News of potential bans, stricter regulations, or crackdowns on cryptocurrency-related activities can trigger market sell-offs and price declines. The regulatory landscape varies across jurisdictions, and regulation changes can have short-term and long-term effects on cryptocurrency prices.

Technological advancements and innovation play a vital role in shaping cryptocurrency prices. Improvements in blockchain technology, scalability solutions, and security measures can enhance the functionality and utility of cryptocurrencies, attracting more users and investors. Positive developments such as implementing new consensus algorithms, privacy enhancements, or interoperability solutions can drive up prices as they demonstrate the potential for real-world applications.

Additionally, the emergence of new use cases and applications within the cryptocurrency ecosystem can significantly impact prices. For example, the rise of decentralized finance (DeFi), non-fungible tokens (NFTs), and blockchain-based gaming platforms has brought increased attention and investment, leading to price appreciation for cryptocurrencies associated with these sectors.

Macroeconomic factors and global events can influence cryptocurrency prices, as they do with traditional financial markets. Cryptocurrencies are not immune to broader economic trends and geopolitical events. Factors such as inflation, interest rates, economic stability, and global crises can impact investor sentiment and risk appetite, which, in turn, can affect cryptocurrency prices.

For instance, during periods of economic uncertainty or financial market volatility, investors may turn to cryptocurrencies as a potential store of value or hedge against traditional markets. This increased demand can drive up cryptocurrency prices. Conversely, positive economic conditions or strong performances in conventional asset classes may divert investment away from cryptocurrencies, leading to price declines.

CHAPTER
II
Getting Started with
Cryptocurrency Trading

Setting Up a Cryptocurrency Wallet

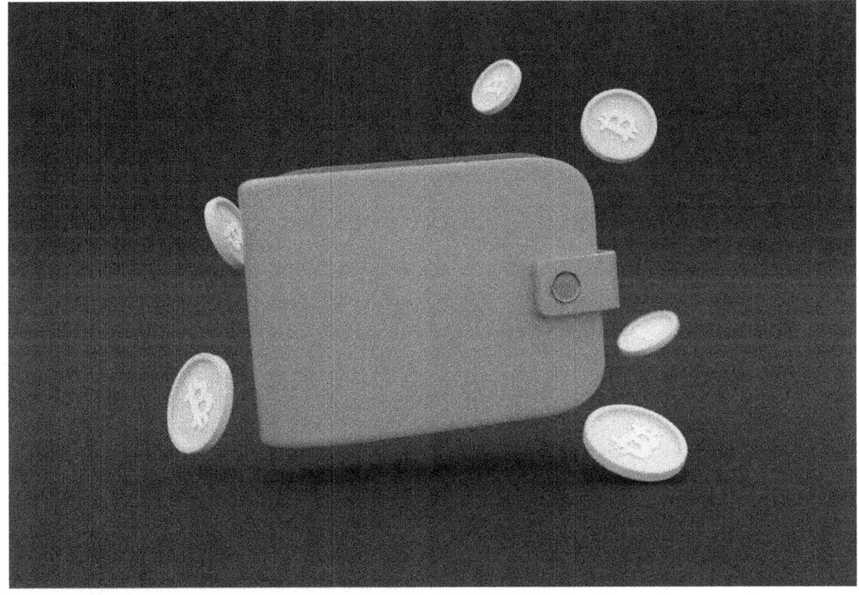

As cryptocurrencies continue gaining popularity, individuals need a secure and reliable means to store and manage their digital assets. This is where cryptocurrency wallets come into play. A digital tool called a cryptocurrency wallet allows users to transmit, receive, and store their cryptocurrency in a secure manner. In this section, we will explore the process of setting up a cryptocurrency wallet, the different types of wallets available, their features, and the importance of security in safeguarding your digital assets.

A cryptocurrency wallet is a software program or hardware device that securely keeps a user's cryptocurrency keys rather than a physical wallet. These keys, consisting of a private key and a public key, are essential for accessing and managing the user's cryptocurrency holdings.

It is important to note that cryptocurrencies themselves are not stored in wallets. Instead, wallets store the cryptographic keys that allow users to access their holdings on the blockchain. Cryptocurrency wallets provide a user-friendly interface that simplifies interacting with the blockchain and managing digital assets.

Cryptocurrency wallets can be broadly categorized into software, hardware, and paper wallets.

Software wallets are digital applications that can be installed on computers, smartphones, or tablets. They offer convenience and accessibility to users. Software wallets can be further categorized into desktop, mobile, and web wallets, each catering to different user preferences and needs.

Desktop wallets are installed and run on personal computers or laptops, giving users complete control over their private keys. Mobile wallets for smartphones and tablets offer on-the-go access to cryptocurrencies. Web wallets are accessible through web browsers and provide the convenience of accessing cryptocurrencies from any device with an internet connection.

Hardware wallets are tangible objects made just for holding cryptocurrency safely. They offer an offline storage solution, keeping the private keys offline and out of reach from potential online threats. One of the safest alternatives accessible, hardware wallets add an additional layer of defense against malware and hacker attempts.

Paper wallets involve generating a pair of public and private keys offline and printing them on a physical piece of paper. Paper wallets are considered a form of cold storage since they are not connected to the internet. They provide a secure option for long-term storage, as the private keys are kept offline, minimizing the risk of online attacks.

Setting up a cryptocurrency wallet varies depending on the type of wallet chosen. However, there are common steps to consider when setting up a wallet:

Before setting up a cryptocurrency wallet, it is important to research different wallets and consider factors such as security features, ease of use, supported cryptocurrencies, and compatibility with your devices. Select a wallet according to your unique requirements and preferences.

For software wallets, visit the chosen wallet's official website or app store and download the application. Follow the installation instructions provided by the wallet provider. Ensure that you download from trusted sources to avoid potential malware or phishing attempts.

Once the wallet is installed, open the application and create a new wallet. This typically involves choosing a strong password or passphrase. Follow the instructions provided by the wallet to complete the setup process. Some wallets may also generate a seed phrase, which is a series of randomly generated words that can be used to recover the wallet in case of loss or device failure.

Creating a backup of your wallet is essential to protect against the loss of private keys or device failure. Follow the wallet's instructions to backup your wallet securely. Backup options include writing down a seed phrase or private key on paper or using encrypted backups on external storage devices. Separate from the device that was used to configure the wallet, keep the backup in a safe and secure area.

To start using your wallet, you need to add cryptocurrencies to it. Obtain the wallet's public address, which serves as your unique identifier on the blockchain, and use it to receive funds from exchanges or other wallets. Follow the wallet's instructions to receive cryptocurrencies.

When creating and utilizing a cryptocurrency wallet, security is of the utmost significance. Cryptocurrencies are inherently secure, but the responsibility of safeguarding private keys lies with the wallet owner. Consider the following security measures:

Choose a strong and unique password for your wallet, combining a mix of uppercase and lowercase letters, numbers, and special characters. When it's feasible, enable two-factor authentication (2FA) to further secure your wallet. 2FA requires another verification step to access the wallet, such as a code sent to your mobile device.

Make sure the software in your wallet is updated. Wallet developers regularly release updates that include security patches and improvements. Keeping your wallet software updated helps protect against potential vulnerabilities and ensures that you have access to the latest security features.

Create regular backups of your wallet and securely store them in offline or encrypted storage. In the event of a lost, stolen, or damaged device, having a backup allows you to recover your wallet and access your funds. Follow the wallet's instructions for backing up and recovering your wallet.

Consider using cold storage options, such as hardware wallets or paper wallets, for long-term storage of significant cryptocurrency holdings. Cold storage keeps private keys offline, significantly reducing the risk of online threats. Hardware wallets, in particular, provide an added layer of security by keeping the private keys isolated from internet-connected devices.

Be cautious of phishing attempts, where malicious actors impersonate legitimate wallet providers or platforms to steal your private keys or login credentials. Always ensure that you access your wallet through official websites or trusted app stores. Double-check website URLs and avoid clicking on suspicious links or providing sensitive information to unknown sources.

Choosing a Cryptocurrency Exchange

In the rapidly evolving world of cryptocurrencies, choosing the right cryptocurrency exchange is crucial for individuals seeking to buy, sell, and trade digital assets. A cryptocurrency exchange serves as an online platform that facilitates the exchange of cryptocurrencies for fiat currencies or other cryptocurrencies. Since there are so many exchanges accessible, each with their own special features and services, it is crucial to carefully consider your demands and make an exchange selection that is in line with your financial objectives. This section will explore the factors to consider when choosing a cryptocurrency exchange, including security, fees, supported cryptocurrencies, liquidity, user experience, and regulatory compliance.

One of the most important things to take into account when picking a cryptocurrency exchange is security. Since exchanges hold users' funds and personal information, opting for platforms with robust security measures in place is crucial. Look for exchanges implementing industry-standard security protocols, such as two-factor authentication (2FA), cold storage of funds, encryption, and regular security audits. Additionally, consider exchanges with a track record of operating without major security breaches and a transparent approach to addressing security vulnerabilities.

Another essential aspect to consider is the fee structure and trading costs associated with the exchange. Exchanges typically charge fees on trades, deposits, and withdrawals. It is critical to comprehend the fee structure and determine whether it fits with your trading volume and investment strategy because these fees can vary greatly between exchanges. Look for exchanges with competitive fees that offer a transparent fee schedule, as excessive fees can significantly impact your trading profitability.

The range of cryptocurrencies supported by an exchange is another crucial consideration. Bitcoin and Ethereum are widely available on most exchanges, but if you are interested in trading less mainstream cryptocurrencies, it is important to choose an exchange that offers a diverse selection. Research the exchange's list of supported cryptocurrencies and ensure it includes the assets you intend to trade or invest in. Additionally, consider whether the exchange regularly adds new cryptocurrencies to its offering, as this can indicate a commitment to staying up-to-date with market trends and providing users with a broader range of options.

Liquidity is the ease with which a cryptocurrency can be purchased or sold without significantly impacting its price. Opting for an exchange with high liquidity ensures that you can execute trades quickly and at fair prices. Higher liquidity also reduces the risk of encountering slippage, where the executed price deviates significantly from the expected price due to low liquidity. Consider exchanges that have a large user base, active trading volume, and a wide range of trading pairs, as these factors contribute to higher liquidity levels.

A user-friendly interface and intuitive user experience are crucial for seamless trading and a positive overall experience on a cryptocurrency exchange. Consider the platform's design, navigation, and ease of use when evaluating exchanges. Look for exchanges that offer clear and intuitive trading interfaces, easy deposit and withdrawal processes, comprehensive order book information, and real-time market data. Additionally, consider whether the exchange provides mobile applications or responsive web interfaces, as this can enhance accessibility and allow for trading on the go.

Regulatory compliance is an important consideration when choosing a cryptocurrency exchange. Exchanges operating within their jurisdictions' legal framework are more likely to offer a secure and reliable trading environment. Research the exchange's compliance with relevant regulations and its approach to Know Your Customer (KYC) and Anti-Money Laundering (AML) procedures. Consider whether the exchange has obtained necessary licenses and has a transparent approach to regulatory compliance. Additionally, evaluate the exchange's reputation within the cryptocurrency community by reading user reviews, assessing its history, and considering any past regulatory or security incidents.

Reliable customer support is crucial in the cryptocurrency exchange space, as technical issues and concerns may arise during trading activities. Consider the availability and responsiveness of customer support channels offered by the exchange. Look for exchanges that provide multiple support options, like live chat, email, or phone support. Additionally, evaluate the exchange's reputation for promptly addressing customer issues and resolving queries. Reliability is also important, as an exchange with frequent downtime or system issues can hinder your trading activities and potentially lead to financial losses.

KYC and Security Measures

The necessity of putting strong security measures and Know Your Customer (KYC) processes in place is becoming more and more important as cryptocurrencies gain popularity. In order to prevent fraud, money laundering, and other illegal actions, businesses must verify the identities of their clients through a procedure known as KYC. In the cryptocurrency space, KYC measures are essential for creating a secure and compliant environment that protects users and ensures the integrity of transactions. In this section, we will explore the significance of KYC and the various security measures employed in the cryptocurrency industry, including identity verification, anti-money laundering protocols, data privacy, and user protection.

When using cryptocurrency platforms, exchanges, or services, KYC procedures require individuals to provide identification documents and personal information to verify their identities. These measures deter criminal activities and ensure compliance with regulatory frameworks. By implementing KYC protocols, cryptocurrency businesses can establish a level of trust and credibility, mitigating risks associated with money laundering, terrorist financing, and other illicit activities.

Identity verification is a critical component of KYC procedures. It involves verifying the authenticity of users' identities by requesting specific documents, such as government-issued identification cards, passports, or utility bills. Cryptocurrency platforms and exchanges require users to submit these documents to confirm their identities before engaging in transactions or accessing certain services.

Advanced user authentication methods, such as two-factor authentication (2FA), strengthen security by requiring users to provide additional verification factors beyond passwords. This increases the platform's overall security and adds another layer of protection against unwanted account access.

Combating the Financing of Terrorism (CFT) as well as Anti-Money Laundering (AML) legislation apply to cryptocurrency enterprises in order to prevent money laundering and financing illegal activities. AML policies involve monitoring transactions, identifying suspicious activities, and reporting them to relevant authorities. Cryptocurrency exchanges and platforms employ transaction monitoring systems and compliance officers to identify and report any potentially suspicious transactions.

CFT measures aim to prevent funds from being used to finance terrorism or illegal activities. Cryptocurrency businesses conduct due diligence to ensure that their services are not used by individuals or entities associated with terrorism or illicit activities. By implementing comprehensive AML and CFT measures, cryptocurrency businesses contribute to the overall security and integrity of the financial system.

Data privacy is a crucial aspect of KYC and security measures in the cryptocurrency industry. Cryptocurrency businesses must handle users' personal information responsibly and protect it from unauthorized access, misuse, or theft. Privacy policies and encryption techniques help safeguard sensitive user data and ensure compliance with data protection regulations.

To enhance privacy, some cryptocurrency projects employ privacy-focused technologies, such as zero-knowledge proofs or cryptographic techniques, which allow for secure and private transactions. These technologies aim to balance privacy and regulatory compliance, enabling users to protect their identities while adhering to KYC requirements.

Ensuring user protection and asset security is paramount in the cryptocurrency industry. Exchanges and platforms employ various security measures to safeguard user funds, including cold storage solutions, multi-signature wallets, and robust encryption algorithms. Cold storage involves storing cryptocurrencies offline, making them less vulnerable to hacking attempts. Multi-signature wallets give an additional degree of security against unauthorized access by requiring multiple signatures to approve transactions.

Additionally, exchanges invest in cybersecurity infrastructure to protect against hacking attempts and data breaches. Penetration testing, vulnerability assessments, and security audits on a regular basis assist identify and address any potential security vulnerabilities. By implementing these measures, exchanges strive to protect user funds and provide a secure trading environment.

Regulatory compliance is essential in the cryptocurrency space to ensure the integrity of transactions and protect users. Cryptocurrency businesses must adhere to the regulations and guidelines set by regulatory bodies in their jurisdictions. Compliance with KYC and AML regulations fosters a secure environment and helps legitimize the cryptocurrency industry in the eyes of regulators, financial institutions, and the general public.

Industry standards also play a significant role in enhancing security in the cryptocurrency space. Organizations like Financial Action Task Force (FATF) and the Blockchain Transparency Institute (BTI) establish guidelines and best practices to promote industry security, transparency, and trust. Adhering to these standards helps foster a healthy and secure cryptocurrency ecosystem.

While security measures and KYC protocols are essential, it is also crucial to strike a balance with user experience. Lengthy or complex KYC processes may deter users from engaging with cryptocurrency platforms. To address this, businesses strive to streamline the KYC process, making it user-friendly and efficient without compromising security.

Cryptocurrency businesses can also explore decentralized identity solutions and self-sovereign identity frameworks, where users control their identities and personal data. These technologies aim to provide a secure, privacy-enhancing alternative to traditional centralized KYC processes, ensuring a better user experience while maintaining robust security measures.

Types of Cryptocurrency Orders

Cryptocurrency trading has gained significant traction in recent years, with a multitude of investors and traders participating in the digital asset market. To navigate this dynamic market successfully, it is essential to understand the various types of cryptocurrency orders available. A cryptocurrency order is an instruction given by a trader to a cryptocurrency exchange, specifying the desired trade parameters. In this section, we will explore the different types of cryptocurrency orders, including market orders, limit orders, stop orders, and more. Understanding these order types will empower traders to execute trades efficiently and effectively.

A market order is the simplest and most common type of cryptocurrency order. With a market order, a trader instructs the exchange to buy or sell a specified amount of cryptocurrency at the best available price in the market. Market orders prioritize execution speed over price, aiming to fill the order as quickly as possible. Market orders are beneficial in highly liquid markets when immediate execution is essential.

The price at which a trader is willing to purchase or sell a cryptocurrency can be specified using limit orders. Unlike market orders, limit orders prioritize price over execution speed. When placing a buy limit order, the trader states a maximum price they are willing to pay, and the order will only execute if the market reaches or falls below that price. Conversely, when placing a sell limit order, the trader specifies a minimum price they are willing to accept, and the order will only execute if the market reaches or exceeds that price.

Limit orders provide control over trade execution and can be beneficial in volatile markets or when traders have specific price targets in mind. However, there is no assurance that the limit order will be executed, as the market may not reach the specified price.

Stop orders, also known as stop-loss orders or stop-limit orders, are designed to limit potential losses or protect profits. A stop order becomes a market order when the specified trigger price is reached. There are two types of stop orders:

A stop-loss order is placed below the current market price for sell orders or above the current market price for buy orders. Suppose the market reaches or falls below the specified trigger price. In that case, a market order is executed, allowing traders to limit potential losses by automatically selling their holdings or entering a buy order to close a short position.

A stop-limit order is similar to a stop-loss order but with an added limit price. When the trigger price is reached, a limit order is placed instead of a market order. The limit order specifies the desired price at which the trader wants to purchase or sell the cryptocurrency. Stop-limit orders provide additional control over the execution price but may not be filled if the market moves quickly or gaps occur.

Stop orders are valuable risk management tools and can help traders protect their investments during market downturns or volatile periods.

Trailing stop orders are dynamic orders that allow traders to set a trailing stop price that follows the market's movements. Trailing stop orders are typically used to protect profits in an upward trending market or limit losses in a downward trending market. The trailing stop price adjusts as the market price shifts in the trader's favor.

For example, if a trader sets a trailing stop order with a 5% trailing percentage, the stop price will trail 5% below the highest price achieved since placing the order. If the market price retraces by 5% from its highest point, the trailing stop order will be triggered and execute a market order.

Trailing stop orders allow traders to lock in profits while still participating in the potential upside of the market. It is important to keep in mind, nevertheless, that due to market volatility, trailing stop orders do not always ensure execution at the exact trailing stop price.

Fill or kill (FOK) orders are designed to ensure immediate and complete execution of a trade or cancel the order entirely. With a FOK order, if the specified quantity cannot be immediately filled in its entirety, the order is canceled, and no partial execution takes place. FOK orders are beneficial when traders want to execute trades quickly and efficiently, with no partial fills or lingering open orders.

Immediate or cancel (IOC) orders are similar to FOK orders but allow for partial execution if the full order cannot be immediately filled. If a portion of an IOC order can be immediately filled, that portion is executed, while any unfilled portion is canceled. IOC orders are useful when traders want to maximize the chances of immediate execution while being willing to accept partial fills.

Good 'til canceled (GTC) orders remain active until they are
manually canceled by the trader or until they are executed. GTC
orders do not have an expiration date and remain on the order book
until filled or canceled. GTC orders are suitable for traders who want
to place long-term orders or take advantage of specific price levels
that may not be immediately achievable.

CHAPTER
III
Fundamental Analysis for Cryptocurrency Trading

Introduction to Fundamental Analysis

Fundamental analysis is a critical methodology in the financial markets to evaluate investments, including cryptocurrencies. It involves assessing the intrinsic value of an asset by analyzing its underlying factors, such as financial performance, industry trends, and market dynamics. In the world of cryptocurrencies, where volatility and speculation are prevalent, fundamental analysis provides a systematic approach to understanding digital assets' long-term viability and potential growth. This section will explore the foundations of fundamental analysis, its key components, and its relevance in evaluating cryptocurrency investments.

A way of assessing an investment based on the intrinsic worth of an asset is fundamental analysis. It analyzes the fundamental factors influencing the asset's value over time. In the context of cryptocurrencies, fundamental analysis involves assessing various aspects, including the technology behind the cryptocurrency, the team behind the project, the utility and adoption of the cryptocurrency, regulatory and legal factors, and market demand.

Unlike technical analysis, which relies on historical price patterns and market data, fundamental analysis aims to understand the underlying value drivers of an asset. By examining these factors, investors can make informed decisions based on a cryptocurrency's potential long-term value and growth prospects.

One of the key components of fundamental analysis is evaluating the technology behind the cryptocurrency and the team behind the project. This includes understanding the blockchain infrastructure, consensus mechanisms, scalability, security features, and innovation potential. Additionally, assessing the development team's experience, expertise, and commitment to the project is vital, as it can influence the successful execution and future development of the cryptocurrency.

Another crucial component is analyzing the market demand and adoption of a cryptocurrency. Factors to consider include user adoption, network effects, partnerships with industry players, and integration with existing financial systems. Assessing the cryptocurrency's utility and its ability to solve real-world problems can provide insights into its long-term prospects.

Financial performance and economic factors also play a significant role in fundamental analysis. This involves evaluating the cryptocurrency project's revenue streams, funding sources, and profitability. Understanding economic factors such as inflation, interest rates, and macroeconomic trends can also impact the valuation of cryptocurrencies, as they can influence investor sentiment and the overall market dynamics.

Additionally, analyzing the regulatory and legal landscape surrounding cryptocurrencies is essential. This includes assessing the regulatory framework, government policies, and legal risks associated with cryptocurrencies. Compliance with anti-money laundering and know-your-customer regulations, security regulations, and taxation policies can affect the cryptocurrency's adoption and overall market sentiment.

Investors rely on various data sources and research methods to conduct fundamental analysis. These include examining the cryptocurrency's whitepaper, technical documentation, and project updates to gain insights into its underlying technology, use cases, and development roadmap. Analyzing financial statements and disclosures, such as audited reports and financial disclosures provided by the cryptocurrency project, helps assess its financial health, revenue sources, and potential for growth.

Market research and industry analysis provide valuable information about market trends, competition, and potential risks and opportunities within the cryptocurrency sector. Staying updated with relevant news, media coverage, and industry publications also helps investors understand the broader market sentiment, regulatory developments, and significant events that can impact the cryptocurrency's value.

While fundamental analysis is a valuable tool for evaluating investments, it also faces some limitations and challenges in the cryptocurrency market. Cryptocurrencies are relatively new assets, and historical data may be limited, making it challenging to assess a cryptocurrency project's long-term performance and reliability. The cryptocurrency market is known for its high volatility and speculative nature, where factors beyond fundamental analysis, such as market sentiment and investor behavior can influence price movements.

Cryptocurrencies' decentralized and pseudonymous nature can make it difficult to obtain complete and accurate information about projects, posing challenges in assessing the credibility and trustworthiness of cryptocurrency teams and their claims. Furthermore, the evolving regulatory landscape surrounding cryptocurrencies introduces uncertainty and potential risks, making it challenging to predict long-term outcomes.

To overcome the limitations of fundamental analysis in the cryptocurrency market, many investors employ a multi-dimensional approach that combines fundamental analysis with other methodologies. This includes incorporating technical analysis, sentiment analysis, and market trend analysis to gain a comprehensive understanding of the cryptocurrency market.

Technical analysis examines historical price patterns, chart patterns, and trading indicators to identify potential entry and exit points for trades. Sentiment analysis involves assessing market sentiment and social media sentiment to gauge the collective mood and perception of the cryptocurrency community. Market trend analysis identifies broader market trends and cyclical patterns to make informed investment decisions.

By integrating different analytical approaches, investors can complement fundamental analysis and make more well-rounded investment decisions in the dynamic and rapidly evolving cryptocurrency market.

Evaluating Project Fundamentals

Evaluating the fundamentals of a cryptocurrency project is a critical step in making informed investment decisions. Project fundamentals refer to the underlying factors that drive a cryptocurrency's value and long-term prospects. These factors include the technology, team, roadmap, community, partnerships, use cases, and market demand. By conducting a thorough analysis of project fundamentals, investors can gain valuable insights into a cryptocurrency's potential growth and viability. This section will explore the key components of evaluating project fundamentals and discuss their significance in assessing cryptocurrency investments.

The technology behind a cryptocurrency project is a crucial aspect to evaluate. This includes the underlying blockchain infrastructure, consensus mechanisms, scalability solutions, and security features. Assessing a project's technological robustness and innovation potential helps determine its ability to solve real-world problems, handle transaction volumes, and adapt to future demands. Additionally, evaluating the project's commitment to ongoing research and development is essential, as continuous improvement and innovation are key drivers of long-term success in the dynamic cryptocurrency ecosystem.

The competence and experience of the development team and project leadership significantly impact the success of a cryptocurrency project. Evaluating the team's expertise, track record, and their ability to execute the project's vision is crucial. Researching the team members' backgrounds, qualifications, and involvement in the cryptocurrency community can provide insights into their capabilities and dedication to the project. Furthermore, understanding the project's governance structure and decision-making processes helps assess the team's transparency and accountability level.

A well-defined roadmap is an important indicator of a cryptocurrency project's commitment to its vision and goals. Evaluating the roadmap helps determine the project's progress, timeline for key milestones, and alignment with the broader market trends. Analyzing the achievement of past milestones and the clarity of future objectives provides insights into the project's execution capabilities and its ability to deliver on its promises.

The strength and engagement of a cryptocurrency project's community play a significant role in its success. Assessing the community's size, activity level, and enthusiasm can provide insights into the project's potential for widespread adoption. Monitoring community forums, social media channels, and developer communities helps gauge the project's sentiment, involvement, and overall support. Additionally, evaluating the project's partnerships with other industry players and its integration into existing systems or platforms can further indicate its adoption potential.

Understanding the practical use cases and market demand for a cryptocurrency is essential. Evaluating the real-world applications and industries that can benefit from the project's technology helps assess its potential for widespread adoption. Researching the target market, competition, and potential growth opportunities provides insights into the market demand and the project's competitive advantages. Evaluating the scalability of the project's solutions and their ability to address existing market inefficiencies or pain points is crucial in determining the cryptocurrency's long-term viability and value proposition.

Compliance with regulatory frameworks and legal considerations is a vital factor to evaluate in a cryptocurrency project. Analyzing the project's adherence to anti-money laundering (AML) and know-your-customer (KYC) regulations helps ensure its compliance with legal requirements and its ability to operate within established financial systems. Understanding the project's approach to data privacy, security regulations, and intellectual property protection is also essential in assessing its risk profile and long-term sustainability.

Evaluating the financial aspects of a cryptocurrency project is crucial to assess its viability and long-term sustainability. Analyzing the project's funding sources, revenue generation strategies, and financial disclosures provides insights into its financial health and ability to fund ongoing development. Furthermore, assessing the project's tokenomics, token distribution model, and potential for value accrual helps determine the incentives for token holders and the overall economic sustainability of the project.

Conducting a comprehensive risk assessment is a vital part of evaluating project fundamentals. Identifying and understanding the potential risks associated with a cryptocurrency project allows investors to make informed decisions. Risks can include technological vulnerabilities, regulatory uncertainties, market competition, governance issues, and potential security breaches. Evaluating risk management strategies, contingency plans, and the project's ability to adapt to changing market conditions provides insights into the project's resilience and ability to navigate challenges.

Assessing Market Adoption and Partnerships

Market adoption and strategic partnerships are critical factors in determining cryptocurrencies' success and long-term viability.

Market adoption refers to the acceptance and utilization of a cryptocurrency by individuals, businesses, and the broader market ecosystem. Partnerships involve collaborations between cryptocurrency projects and other industry players, such as businesses, financial institutions, and technology providers. Evaluating market adoption and partnerships provides valuable insights into a cryptocurrency's growth potential, utility, and integration opportunities. This section will explore the significance of market adoption and partnerships in the cryptocurrency industry and discuss key indicators for evaluating their impact on a cryptocurrency's success.

Market adoption is a vital factor in determining the success of a cryptocurrency. Evaluating the user base and adoption rate provides insights into the cryptocurrency's utility, demand, and potential for growth. Assessing user growth, transaction volume, merchant acceptance, and geographic reach are key indicators for evaluating market adoption. Monitoring the growth rate of active users, wallets, or addresses associated with a cryptocurrency helps gauge its popularity and increase acceptance. Analyzing the transaction volume on the blockchain network provides insights into the level of activity and utilization of the cryptocurrency. Evaluating the number of merchants and businesses accepting cryptocurrency as a form of payment demonstrates its practical use in everyday transactions. Assessing the geographic distribution of users and adoption rates helps evaluate the cryptocurrency's global reach and potential for expansion.

The presence of real-world use cases strongly indicates a cryptocurrency's value and adoption potential. Evaluating the practical applications and industries that benefit from cryptocurrency provides insights into its utility and relevance. Key considerations are assessing industry adoption, efficiency gains, and decentralized applications (dApps) built on the cryptocurrency's blockchain platform. Identifying industries or sectors that have embraced the cryptocurrency and are actively using it in their operations demonstrates its practicality and potential for integration. Evaluating how the cryptocurrency streamlines processes, reduces costs, or enhances efficiency within specific industries highlights its value proposition and potential for widespread adoption. Analyzing the number and quality of dApps built on the cryptocurrency's blockchain platform indicates its ecosystem's vibrancy and ability to support decentralized applications.

Strategic partnerships play a crucial role in expanding the reach and utility of a cryptocurrency. Evaluating partnerships provides insights into integration opportunities, industry support, and the project's credibility. Assessing industry collaborations, exchange listings, and technology partnerships are key considerations. Partnerships with established companies, financial institutions, or technology providers demonstrate industry recognition and validation. Collaborations that enable real-world use cases or bring additional resources to the project enhance its growth potential. Being listed on reputable cryptocurrency exchanges improves liquidity and accessibility for investors. Evaluating the number and quality of exchanges where the cryptocurrency is listed helps evaluate its market presence. Collaborations with technology companies or blockchain platforms can enhance the cryptocurrency's functionality, scalability, or security. Partnerships that leverage complementary strengths can drive innovation and improve the project's competitive advantage.

Adhering to regulatory frameworks and compliance standards is crucial for cryptocurrencies to gain wider acceptance. Evaluating a cryptocurrency's regulatory compliance provides insights into its long-term sustainability and potential barriers to adoption. Key considerations include assessing compliance with anti-money laundering (AML) and know-your-customer (KYC) regulations, regulatory approvals, and legal clarity. Compliance with AML and KYC regulations demonstrates the project's commitment to legal and regulatory requirements. Any approvals or licenses obtained from regulatory authorities or government bodies indicate compliance with local regulations and facilitate market entry and acceptance. Understanding the legal status of cryptocurrency in different jurisdictions helps identify potential risks and legal uncertainties that could affect adoption and market sentiment.

A strong and engaged community can significantly impact the success and adoption of a cryptocurrency. Assessing community engagement provides insights into user loyalty, support, and the project's ability to foster collaboration. Key indicators include evaluating social media presence, developer community, governance and voting mechanisms, and community initiatives. Analyzing the size and activity level of the cryptocurrency's social media channels, forums, and community platforms helps gauge community engagement and sentiment. The size and involvement of the cryptocurrency's developer community indicate the level of innovation, support, and potential for ecosystem growth. Assessing the community's involvement in governance decisions and the transparency of voting mechanisms highlights decentralization and community empowerment within the project. Community-driven initiatives, events, and collaborations demonstrate the project's ability to foster engagement and generate grassroots support.

The accessibility and user experience of a cryptocurrency significantly impact its adoption. Evaluating the user interface, wallet solutions, and overall user experience helps determine its appeal to a broader audience. Assessing wallet solutions, user-friendly interfaces, and scalability are key considerations. The availability and functionality of user-friendly wallet solutions simplify the onboarding process and enhance user convenience. Intuitive interfaces and straightforward processes make it easier for users to interact with the cryptocurrency, increasing adoption among non-technical users. Evaluating the cryptocurrency's ability to handle many transactions efficiently ensures a smooth user experience and prevents congestion on the network.

News and Events Impacting Cryptocurrency Prices

News and events profoundly impact the cryptocurrency market, often causing significant price fluctuations. Investors and traders closely monitor the latest developments, as news about regulatory changes, technological advancements, adoption by major companies, security breaches, and economic indicators can shape investor sentiment and influence market dynamics. Understanding the relationship between news and events and their impact on cryptocurrency prices is crucial for making informed investment decisions. In this section, we will explore the various types of news and events that can impact cryptocurrency prices, analyze their significance, and discuss strategies for navigating this dynamic landscape.

Regulatory news and developments can have a substantial impact on cryptocurrency prices. When governments introduce new regulations, policies, or issue statements regarding cryptocurrencies, it creates uncertainty within the market. News of a country implementing strict regulations or outright bans on cryptocurrency-related activities often leads to a decline in prices, as investors become apprehensive about the future of the asset class. Conversely, positive regulatory developments, such as recognizing cryptocurrencies as legal tender or introducing favorable regulations, can boost prices and instill confidence among investors.

Technological advancements and innovations within the cryptocurrency industry can significantly impact prices. News about upgrades to existing blockchain protocols, developing scalable solutions, or launching new features can generate positive sentiment and drive higher prices. Investors often view these advancements as signs of progress and increased utility, leading to increased demand for cryptocurrency. Additionally, announcements regarding partnerships between blockchain projects and technology companies can create positive market buzz, signaling potential integration opportunities and driving prices upward.

News of major companies integrating cryptocurrencies into their operations or accepting them as a form of payment can profoundly impact cryptocurrency prices. Such announcements validate cryptocurrencies' utility and mainstream acceptance, attracting more investors to the asset class. When well-known retailers or financial institutions declare their intention to accept cryptocurrencies, it generates positive sentiment and drives up demand. The increased adoption and integration by major companies are strong indicators of cryptocurrency acceptance and potential future growth.

Security breaches and hacking incidents within the cryptocurrency ecosystem can have a detrimental effect on prices. News of a significant exchange hack or a vulnerability in a popular cryptocurrency wallet erodes investor confidence and leads to a sharp price decline. These events often prompt investors to sell off their holdings, fearing further security risks. The negative publicity surrounding security breaches highlights the vulnerabilities of the cryptocurrency ecosystem and creates a sense of uncertainty among market participants. Conversely, news about improved security measures or successful mitigation of a security incident can restore confidence and stabilize prices.

News and events related to economic indicators, market sentiment, and broader financial trends can impact cryptocurrency prices. For instance, news of a global economic recession or geopolitical tensions can drive investors towards safe-haven assets like cryptocurrencies, increasing demand and pushing prices higher. Positive market sentiment towards digital assets, adoption by institutional investors, or news of favorable regulatory developments can fuel buying interest and result in price appreciation. Conversely, negative news about the broader financial markets or a decline in investor confidence can decrease cryptocurrency prices.

Investors should adopt strategic approaches to navigate the impact of news and events on cryptocurrency prices. Key strategies include:

It's crucial to keep educated and use reliable information sources. Trustworthy news outlets, official project announcements, and reputable industry publications can provide accurate and timely information to make informed decisions.

Understanding market sentiment is crucial when assessing the impact of news on cryptocurrency prices. Monitoring social media discussions, sentiment analysis tools, and market sentiment indicators can provide insights into the collective mood of investors and traders.

Some news and events have short-term effects on cryptocurrency prices, while others can shape long-term trends. It is important to differentiate between temporary price fluctuations driven by short-term news and fundamental shifts that can impact the cryptocurrency's value over an extended period.

Diversification is a key strategy to manage the impact of news and events on cryptocurrency prices. By spreading investments across different cryptocurrencies and asset classes, investors can mitigate the risk associated with price volatility driven by specific news or events.

Fundamental analysis, which involves assessing a cryptocurrency's underlying value and long-term prospects, can help investors make informed decisions beyond short-term news-driven price movements. By evaluating technology, team, adoption, and market demand, investors can identify cryptocurrencies with strong fundamentals that are more likely to withstand market fluctuations.

CHAPTER
IV
Technical Analysis for
Cryptocurrency Trading

Introduction to Technical Analysis

Technical analysis is a widely used approach in financial markets, including cryptocurrency, to analyze price trends, identify patterns, and make informed investment decisions. It involves the study of historical market data, primarily price and volume, to predict future price movements. By examining charts, patterns, and indicators, technical analysts aim to gain insights into market psychology and identify potential opportunities for buying or selling cryptocurrencies. This section will explore the fundamentals of technical analysis, its key concepts, and the significance of using this approach in the cryptocurrency market.

Technical analysis is founded on three core principles: the market discounts everything, price moves in trends, and history tends to repeat itself. The underlying assumption is that all relevant information impacting a cryptocurrency's price is already reflected in its historical price movements. Technical analysts interpret these historical price patterns to predict future price movements. They believe that markets move in trends, and by identifying these trends, they can make better investment decisions.

Charting tools and patterns are central to technical analysis. Visual representations of price fluctuations over a specified period are offered by numerous chart types, including line charts, bar charts, and candlestick charts. Trendlines, support and resistance levels, and chart formations are examples of patterns that aid analysts in identifying future price reversals or continuations. For example, a head and shoulders pattern may indicate a potential trend reversal, while a triangle pattern may suggest a consolidation phase before a significant breakout.

Trend analysis is a crucial aspect of technical analysis. Trends represent the general direction in which a cryptocurrency's price moves over a specific period. Technical analysts identify three types of trends: uptrends, downtrends, and sideways trends. Uptrends occur when prices form higher highs and higher lows, indicating a bullish market. Downtrends occur when prices form lower highs and lower lows, indicating a bearish market. Sideways trends occur when prices move within a range, indicating a lack of a clear trend.

Technical indicators are mathematical calculations applied to price and volume data to generate additional insights into market trends and potential reversals. These indicators help traders and investors confirm their analysis or identify possible entry and exit points. Moving averages, relative strength index (RSI), stochastic oscillators, as well as MACD (moving average convergence divergence) are common technical indicators used in cryptocurrency trading. Each indicator provides unique information about the strength of a trend, overbought or oversold conditions, and potential market reversals.

Support and resistance levels are important concepts in technical analysis. Support refers to a price level at which buying pressure is expected to outweigh selling pressure, preventing prices from falling further. On the other hand, resistance refers to a price level at which selling pressure is expected to outweigh buying pressure, preventing prices from rising further. These levels are identified by analyzing historical price movements and are considered key areas where price reversals or breakouts may occur.

Volume analysis plays a crucial role in technical analysis. Volume represents the number of shares or units of a cryptocurrency traded within a given period. Analyzing volume helps traders and investors understand the strength and confirmation of price movements. Increased volume during an uptrend suggests a stronger buying pressure, while increased volume during a downtrend indicates a stronger selling pressure. Divergence between price and volume can also provide valuable insights into potential market reversals.

Technical analysis can be applied to different timeframes, ranging from intraday trading to long-term investing. Depending on their preferred timeframes and risk tolerance, traders and investors employ different trading techniques, such as scalping, day trading, swing trading, and position trading. Shorter timeframes are often associated with more frequent trading and focus on smaller price movements, while longer timeframes consider broader market trends and aim for larger price targets.

While technical analysis has gained popularity, it has limitations and criticisms. Critics argue that technical analysis is subjective and prone to bias, as different analysts may interpret the same chart differently. They also highlight the "self-fulfilling prophecy" phenomenon, where widespread adoption of certain technical patterns or indicators leads to their own effectiveness. Additionally, technical analysis does not consider fundamental factors such as market news, company financials, or broader economic indicators, which can also influence cryptocurrency prices.

To make well-rounded investment decisions, integrating technical analysis with other approaches, such as fundamental and market sentiment analysis, is often beneficial. A cryptocurrency's intrinsic value is determined by performing a fundamental analysis on its technology, team, adoption, and market demand. Market sentiment analysis evaluates investors' overall mood and perception, which can impact short-term price movements. By combining these approaches, traders and investors can comprehensively understand the cryptocurrency market and make more informed decisions.

Common Technical Indicators and Oscillators

Technical analysis relies on various tools and indicators to gain insights into market trends, momentum, and potential trading opportunities. These indicators help traders and investors make informed decisions based on historical price and volume data. This section will explore some of the most common technical indicators and oscillators used in financial markets, including the cryptocurrency market. By understanding these indicators and their interpretations, market participants can enhance their trading strategies and navigate the dynamic landscape of the financial markets more effectively.

Moving averages are frequently used to determine a trend's direction and smooth out price swings. A moving average calculates the average price over a specific period, updating with each new data point. Simple moving averages (SMA) and exponential moving averages (EMA) are two forms of moving averages that traders frequently employ. SMAs assign equal weight to all data points, while EMAs give more weight to recent prices, making them more responsive to short-term changes. Moving averages can signal trend reversals when shorter-term moving averages cross above or below longer-term moving averages.

Popular oscillators like the Relative Strength Index (RSI) examine the size and speed of recent price fluctuations to determine if an asset is overbought or oversold. The range of the RSI is 0 to 100, with readings above 70 denoting overbought situations and below 30 denoting oversold ones. Traders use RSI to identify potential trend reversals or confirm the strength of an existing trend. The divergence between price and RSI can also provide insights into market momentum and potential reversals.

A versatile indicator that combines moving averages with oscillators is known as Moving Average Convergence Divergence (MACD). It consists of the MACD line and the signal line, along with a histogram representing the difference between the two lines. The MACD line is calculated by subtracting the longer-term EMA from the shorter-term EMA, while the signal line is typically a 9-day EMA of the MACD line. Traders use MACD crossovers, where the MACD line crosses above or below the signal line, to identify potential trend reversals and generate buy or sell signals.

Stochastic Oscillator is a momentum indicator that evaluates a cryptocurrency's closing price in relation to its price range over a given time frame. The oscillator consists of two lines: the %K line, which represents the current closing price relative to the range, and the %D line, which is a moving average of the %K line. The Stochastic Oscillator, which has a scale from 0 to 100, measures probable trend reversals, overbought and oversold positions, and other market variables. When the %K line crosses above the %D line in oversold territory, it generates a bullish signal, while a cross below the %D line in overbought territory suggests a bearish signal.

A moving average (usually a 20-day SMA) and two standard deviation bands placed above and below the moving average make up Bollinger Bands. These bands expand and contract based on market volatility. When prices approach the upper band, it suggests overbought conditions, while prices nearing the lower band indicate oversold conditions. Traders use Bollinger Bands to assess volatility and identify potential price breakouts. Breakouts occur when prices move outside the bands, indicating a potential continuation or reversal of the current trend.

Based on the Fibonacci sequence, the Fibonacci retracement is a method used to identify probable support and resistance levels. Traders plot Fibonacci retracement levels on a price chart by identifying significant price swings and drawing horizontal lines at key Fibonacci levels (such as 38.2%, 50%, and 61.8%). These levels often act as areas of support or resistance, where price reversals or significant price movements may occur. Fibonacci retracement helps traders identify potential entry or exit points based on the assumption that markets often retrace a portion of a previous price movement before continuing the overall trend.

The Ichimoku Cloud, also known as Ichimoku Kinko Hyo, is a comprehensive indicator that provides insights into market trends, support and resistance levels, and potential trading signals. It consists of several components, including the Kumo (cloud), Tenkan-sen (conversion line), Kijun-sen (baseline), Chikou Span (lagging line), and Senkou Span A and B (leading spans). Traders use the Ichimoku Cloud to identify the direction of the trend, potential support and resistance levels, and signals generated by the interactions between different indicator components.

While each technical indicator or oscillator provides valuable insights into market trends and momentum, combining multiple indicators can enhance the reliability of trading signals. Traders often look for confirmation and confluence, where multiple indicators or oscillators generate similar signals or align with the overall trend. This approach increases the probability of accurate predictions and reduces the impact of false signals.

Chart Patterns and Trend Analysis

Chart patterns and trend analysis are fundamental tools in technical analysis that enable traders and investors to understand market behavior, identify potential opportunities, and make informed trading decisions. By analyzing historical price data and visual patterns on price charts, market participants can gain valuable insights into the psychology of buyers and sellers, market trends, and potential price reversals. In this section, we will explore the significance of chart patterns and trend analysis, examine common chart patterns, and discuss their implications for trading strategies in various financial markets.

Traders can identify possible market trends and forecast future price behavior by using chart patterns, which are visual representations of price movements on charts. These patterns are formed by the interaction between buyers and sellers in the market and reflect the collective sentiment of market participants. Chart patterns are categorized into two main types: reversal and continuation patterns.

Reversal patterns are characterized by a transition from bullish to bearish, or vice versa, and they are used to predict probable changes in the current market direction. Examples of reversal patterns include head and shoulders, double top, and double bottom patterns. Continuation patterns, on the other hand, suggest a temporary pause in the prevailing trend before it resumes. Common continuation patterns include triangles, flags, and pennants.

Trend analysis is a crucial component of technical analysis that focuses on identifying and analyzing market trends. A trend is an overall pattern of price movement for a market or asset over a given time frame. Trends can be categorized as uptrends, downtrends, or sideways trends.

Higher highs and higher lows, which signify a bullish market sentiment, characterize uptrends. On the other hand, Downtrends consist of lower highs and lower lows, indicating a bearish market sentiment. Sideways trends occur when prices move within a horizontal range, with no clear upward or downward bias.

The Head and Shoulders pattern is a widely recognized reversal pattern characterized by three distinct peaks, with the central peak (the head) being the highest, and the other two peaks (the shoulders) flanking it. The pattern is completed by drawing a neckline connecting the lows between the peaks. This pattern suggests a potential trend reversal from bullish to bearish.

Double Top and Double Bottom patterns are reversal patterns characterized by two consecutive peaks (double top) or two consecutive troughs (double bottom) formed at a similar level. These patterns indicate a potential trend reversal and provide trading opportunities.

Triangles are continuation patterns that represent a temporary consolidation phase before the resumption of the prevailing trend. They can be symmetrical, ascending, or descending. A breakout above the upper trendline suggests a bullish continuation, while a breakout below the lower trendline indicates a bearish continuation.

Flags and pennants are continuation patterns after a strong price move. Flags are rectangular patterns that slope against the prevailing trend, while pennants are small symmetrical triangles. The continuation pattern is confirmed by a breakout in the direction of the dominant trend.

Chart patterns and trend analysis provide valuable insights for developing trading strategies. Traders can use chart patterns to identify potential entry and exit points, set stop-loss orders, and manage risk. When a chart pattern is confirmed, traders can establish positions in the direction of the pattern and set price targets based on the pattern's projected move. Traders may also consider additional factors such as volume analysis, support and resistance levels, and the overall market context to strengthen their trading decisions.

Moreover, combining chart patterns with other technical indicators and oscillators can enhance the reliability of trading signals. For example, using trendlines or moving averages in conjunction with chart patterns can help confirm the validity of the pattern and provide additional support or resistance levels.

It is important to note that chart patterns are not foolproof and can sometimes produce false signals. Traders should exercise caution and consider the overall market conditions, risk management principles, and the use of appropriate risk-reward ratios when applying chart patterns to their trading strategies.

Chart patterns and trend analysis can be applied to various timeframes, ranging from intraday trading to long-term investing. Shorter timeframes are often associated with more frequent trading and focus on smaller price movements, while longer timeframes consider broader market trends and aim for larger price targets.

Chart patterns and trend analysis can also be used to analyze a variety of financial markets, including those for stocks, commodities, forex, and cryptocurrencies. While specific patterns may exhibit variations across different markets, the underlying principles remain the same. Traders and investors can adapt their analysis to different markets and develop strategies based on each market's specific characteristics and dynamics.

While chart patterns and trend analysis provide valuable insights into market behavior, they are with limitations and challenges. First, the subjective nature of pattern recognition can introduce interpretation biases among different traders. Second, market conditions can sometimes lead to false breakouts or breakdowns, challenging the reliability of chart patterns. Additionally, volatile or illiquid markets may exhibit less reliable patterns, making it more challenging to generate accurate signals.

To effectively utilize chart patterns and trend analysis, traders should continuously learn and stay updated with evolving market dynamics. Regularly studying price charts, analyzing historical patterns, and observing how patterns unfold in real-time can enhance pattern recognition skills and improve decision-making.

Support and Resistance Levels

Support and resistance levels are fundamental concepts in technical analysis that help traders and investors identify key price levels where buying and selling pressures have historically influenced the market. These levels act as psychological and technical barriers, shaping price movements and providing valuable insights into potential reversals, breakouts, and trend continuation. In this section, we will delve into the significance of support and resistance levels, explore their characteristics and formations, discuss their implications for trading strategies, and highlight techniques to identify and utilize these levels effectively.

Support and resistance levels are horizontal or diagonal price levels that act as barriers to price movement. Support represents a price level at which buying pressure is expected to outweigh selling pressure, preventing prices from falling further. On the other hand, resistance represents a price level at which selling pressure is expected to outweigh buying pressure, preventing prices from rising further.

Supply and demand determine the levels of support and resistance. When the demand for an asset exceeds its supply, prices tend to rise, creating resistance levels as selling pressure increases. Conversely, when the supply exceeds demand, prices tend to fall, leading to the establishment of support levels as buying pressure increases.

The levels of support and resistance can be determined using a variety of methods. Traders analyze historical price data, trendlines, moving averages, and Fibonacci retracement levels to pinpoint potential support and resistance areas. Historical price levels that have previously acted as turning points can indicate the significance of specific levels. Trendlines drawn by connecting significant highs or lows on a price chart can act as dynamic support or resistance levels. Moving averages, such as the 50-day or 200-day moving average, can also act as support or resistance levels. Additionally, Fibonacci retracement levels derived from the Fibonacci sequence help identify potential support and resistance levels based on the proportionate retracement of a previous price move.

Support and resistance levels possess several key characteristics. First, the strength of a support or resistance level is determined by the number of times prices have respected that level and the volume traded near it. Levels that have been tested multiple times with significant price reactions and high trading volume are considered stronger levels. Second, the confirmation of a level's significance increases with the number of times prices have respected it. Multiple touches and bounces off a level validate its credibility as a support or resistance level. Third, once a support level is breached, it often becomes a resistance level, and vice versa. This phenomenon is known as "role reversal" and is a crucial concept in understanding the dynamics of support and resistance levels. Lastly, round numbers, such as $10 or $100, often have psychological significance and can act as support or resistance levels. These levels attract attention from traders and investors, influencing their buying or selling decisions.

Support and resistance levels offer valuable insights for developing trading strategies. Breakouts occur when prices break above a resistance level or below a support level. Traders may enter a trade in the direction of the breakout, expecting further price movement in that direction. Bounces off support or resistance levels indicate the strength of those levels. Traders can consider entering trades when prices bounce off a level, anticipating a continuation of the prevailing trend or a potential reversal. Moreover, support and resistance levels can be used to determine appropriate stop-loss levels and set take-profit targets. Placing stop-loss orders slightly below a support level or above a resistance level can help protect against potential losses if the level is breached. Traders may choose to close their positions or take profits near these levels, as prices often struggle to move beyond them.

To effectively utilize support and resistance levels, traders can employ various techniques. Seeking confirmation from other technical indicators or chart patterns can increase the reliability of the identified levels. Analyzing multiple timeframes helps identify significant levels that align across different timeframes. As support and resistance levels are not static but can change over time, regular reassessment and updating of these levels is necessary. Combining support and resistance levels with other technical indicators, such as trendlines, moving averages, or oscillators, can provide additional confirmation and strengthen trading decisions.

While support and resistance levels are valuable tools, they have limitations. False breakouts occur when prices temporarily breach support or resistance levels before quickly reversing course. Traders should exercise caution and wait for confirmation before entering trades based on potential breakouts. Dynamic market conditions, especially during significant news events or unexpected market shocks, may challenge the reliability of support and resistance levels. Traders should consider the broader market context and adapt their strategies accordingly. Additionally, identifying support and resistance levels involves a degree of subjectivity, as different traders may have varying interpretations of their significance and placement.

Effectively utilizing support and resistance levels requires continuous learning and adaptation. Regularly analyzing price charts, studying historical patterns, and observing how prices interact with identified levels in real-time refine traders' identification skills, improve decision-making, and help them adapt to evolving market conditions.

CHAPTER
V
Developing Cryptocurrency Trading Strategies

Short-term vs. Long-term Trading Strategies

Trading strategies play a crucial role in the financial markets, allowing traders and investors to capitalize on opportunities and achieve their financial goals. One of traders' key decisions is choosing between short-term and long-term trading strategies. Short-term trading focuses on capitalizing on small price movements within a limited time frame, while long-term trading aims to capture larger price trends over an extended period. This section will explore the characteristics, advantages, and challenges of short-term and long-term trading strategies and consider selecting the most suitable approach based on individual goals and risk tolerance.

Short-term trading strategies, also known as day trading or intraday trading, involve opening and closing positions within a single trading day or a few days. Traders who adopt short-term strategies rely on technical analysis, chart patterns, and short-term price fluctuations to make quick trading decisions. They aim to profit from small price movements and exploit market volatility.

Short-term trading strategies offer several advantages. First, they provide the opportunity for frequent trades, enabling traders to take advantage of multiple opportunities within a short time frame. Second, short-term traders can benefit from leveraging the power of compounding by reinvesting their profits in subsequent trades. Third, short-term trading allows for tighter risk management as positions are generally closed before the end of the trading day, minimizing exposure to overnight market risks.

However, short-term trading comes with its own set of challenges. It requires constant monitoring of price movements and quick decision-making, which can be mentally and emotionally demanding. The short time frame also leaves less room for error, as small mistakes can have a significant impact on profitability. Additionally, short-term trading requires access to real-time market data, reliable execution platforms, and efficient trade management systems.

Long-term trading strategies, also known as position trading or trend following, involve holding positions for an extended period, ranging from weeks to years. Long-term traders focus on capturing significant price trends and aim to benefit from long-term market movements. They typically rely on fundamental analysis, economic indicators, and market research to identify undervalued assets and potential catalysts for price appreciation.

Long-term trading strategies offer several advantages. First, they allow traders to capitalize on major price trends, potentially capturing substantial profits. Second, long-term traders are not as susceptible to short-term market noise or temporary price fluctuations. Third, long-term trading requires less time and attention than short-term trading, as positions are held for extended periods.

However, long-term trading also presents challenges. Patience and discipline are essential, as positions may require months or even years to materialize fully. Long-term traders must be comfortable with potential drawdowns or periods of stagnation before the market moves in their favor. Additionally, holding positions for extended periods exposes traders to overnight and systemic risks, including market shocks, economic events, and geopolitical factors.

Choosing between short-term and long-term trading strategies depends on various factors, including individual goals, risk tolerance, time availability, and trading style. It is essential to align the chosen strategy with personal preferences and resources to maximize the chances of success.

Short-term trading may be more suitable for individuals seeking frequent trading opportunities, aiming for quick profits, and comfortable with higher risk levels. On the other hand, long-term trading aligns better with individuals seeking sustainable growth, willing to withstand periods of volatility, and having a more conservative risk appetite.

Short-term trading requires significant time and attention throughout the trading day, as traders monitor price movements and execute trades. Individuals with limited availability may find long-term trading more manageable, as it requires less active involvement and fewer daily monitoring requirements.

Different trading styles may align better with specific time horizons. Aggressive traders who thrive on short-term price fluctuations and enjoy active decision-making may prefer short-term strategies. More patient traders who prefer to ride long-term trends and avoid frequent decision-making may gravitate towards long-term strategies.

Short-term trading often requires more capital to take advantage of smaller price movements due to higher trading frequency and potential transaction costs. Long-term trading may require less capital upfront but necessitates the ability to hold positions for extended periods and withstand potential drawdowns.

Risk management and emotional discipline are critical for successful trading regardless of the chosen strategy. Short-term traders must set strict stop-loss orders, manage position sizes effectively, and avoid impulsive decision-making. Long-term traders should establish realistic profit targets, consider diversification across different asset classes, and maintain a long-term perspective even during periods of market volatility.

In practice, traders often adopt hybrid approaches that combine elements of both short-term and long-term strategies. For example, swing trading involves capturing intermediate price swings within larger trends. Traders may also utilize long-term strategies as a core investment approach while taking advantage of short-term trading opportunities within that broader framework. Flexibility and adaptation are key as market conditions evolve, allowing traders to adjust their strategies based on changing market dynamics.

Successful trading requires continuous learning and evaluation. Traders should regularly review and analyze their trading performance, refine their strategies, and adapt to market conditions. Continuous education, staying updated with financial news and developments, and interacting with other traders can enhance skills and insights.

Day Trading Strategies

Cryptocurrency trading offers various strategies to capitalize on the market's volatility, and day trading has emerged as a popular approach. Day trading enatils opening and closing positions within the same trading day, aiming to profit from short-term price fluctuations. This section will explore the fundamentals of day trading in cryptocurrency markets, including its advantages, key strategies, risk management techniques, and the importance of continuous learning.

Day trading is a short-term trading strategy focused on capturing small price movements within a single trading day. Traders aim to take advantage of intraday volatility by opening and closing positions promptly. The primary objective of day trading is to generate profits from these frequent price fluctuations.

Cryptocurrency markets are known for their inherent volatility, making them attractive to day traders. The frequent price swings create opportunities for quick gains by buying low and selling high within a short period. Day traders often rely on technical analysis, chart patterns, and market indicators to identify favorable entry and exit points.

A strategy called momentum trading involves identifying cryptocurrencies that are experiencing significant price movements or strong upward or downward trends. The goal of traders is to ride the momentum and place trades in the direction of the current trend. Momentum indicators, like Relative Strength Index (RSI) and Moving Average Convergence Divergence (MACD), can assist in identifying these opportunities.

Breakout trading entails identifying key support and resistance levels and entering trades when the price breaks through these levels. Traders look for breakouts above resistance levels to initiate long positions or below support levels to initiate short positions. Volume analysis and chart patterns like triangles or rectangles can help confirm breakout signals.

A strategy called Scalping involves making multiple quick trades throughout the day to capture small price differentials. Traders aim to profit from minor price fluctuations by entering and exiting positions within seconds or minutes. Scalping requires a high concentration level and the ability to act swiftly, relying on technical analysis and order flow data.

Implementing stop-loss orders is crucial in day trading to limit potential losses. Traders set predetermined exit points where their positions are automatically closed if the price moves against them. This helps protect capital and prevents substantial losses in case of unfavorable price movements.

Proper position sizing is essential in day trading to manage risk effectively. Traders allocate a specific percentage of their trading capital to each trade, ensuring that potential losses are within an acceptable range. By controlling position size, traders can limit their exposure to individual trades and protect their overall portfolio.

Evaluating the risk-reward ratio is essential to maintain a favorable balance between potential profits and potential losses. Traders assess the potential profit target against the risk of the trade to determine if it aligns with their risk appetite. Favorable risk-reward ratios ensure that potential gains outweigh potential losses.

Proficiency in technical analysis is essential for day traders. Traders can determine potential entry and exit points by studying chart patterns, trends, and indicators. Learning about different technical analysis tools and their application is crucial for refining trading strategies.

Staying informed about market news, events, and updates is vital for day traders. They should monitor factors impacting cryptocurrency prices, such as regulatory developments, partnerships, and market sentiment. Keeping up-to-date with market analysis and industry trends helps traders make informed decisions.

Day trading requires practice and experience to develop skills and intuition. Traders can utilize demo accounts or paper trading to gain experience without risking real capital. Analyzing past trades, identifying patterns, and learning from mistakes contribute to improving day trading skills.

Swing Trading Strategies

Cryptocurrency markets are known for their volatility, creating opportunities for various trading strategies. One popular approach is swing trading, which involves capturing medium-term price movements by holding positions for several days to weeks. In this section, we will explore the fundamentals of swing trading in cryptocurrency markets, including its advantages, key strategies, risk management techniques, and the importance of adaptability.

A strategy called swing trading seeks to profit from medium-term price changes that are consistent with a cryptocurrency's broader trend. Unlike day trading, swing traders hold positions for a longer period, ranging from a few days to several weeks. The aim is to capture significant price swings during bullish or bearish market conditions.

Swing traders benefit from trending markets by entering positions aligned with the prevailing trend. By holding positions for a longer duration, they can ride the upward or downward momentum, maximizing profit potential. This approach leverages the power of sustained price movements in the market.

Unlike day trading, swing trading requires less time commitment as positions are held for longer periods. Swing traders can effectively manage their trades alongside other commitments, making it suitable for part-time traders or those with limited availability.

Swing trading typically involves fewer transactions compared to day trading, resulting in lower transaction costs. By reducing the frequency of trades, swing traders can save on fees and commissions associated with each transaction, improving overall profitability.

Trend Reversal Trading is a strategy that focuses on identifying potential trend reversals. Swing traders look for price patterns, chart formations, or technical indicators that suggest a change in the prevailing trend. Swing traders aim to profit from the subsequent price movement by entering positions early in the reversal.

Breakout trading is a popular swing trading strategy that identifies key support and resistance levels. Swing traders enter positions when the price breaks above a resistance level or below a support level, anticipating a significant price movement toward the breakout.

Pullback trading involves entering positions during temporary price retracements within an ongoing trend. Swing traders identify a strong trend and wait for a price pullback to a predetermined support or resistance level. They then enter positions in the direction of the prevailing trend, aiming to capture the next leg of the price movement.

Implementing stop-loss orders is essential in swing trading to limit potential losses. Swing traders set predetermined exit points where their positions are automatically closed if the price moves against them. This helps protect capital and manage risk in case the trade does not go as anticipated.

Proper position sizing is crucial in swing trading to manage risk effectively. Traders allocate a specific percentage of their trading capital to each trade, ensuring that potential losses are within an acceptable range. Swing traders maintain a balanced portfolio by adjusting position sizes based on risk tolerance and market conditions.

Swing traders use profit-taking strategies to secure gains as the price moves in their favor. They can employ trailing stop orders or scale out of positions, gradually taking profits as the price reaches predetermined targets. These strategies help lock in profits and minimize the risk of giving back gains during market fluctuations.

Swing traders must remain adaptable and adjust their strategies to changing market conditions. Cryptocurrency markets can experience periods of high volatility, low volatility, or even range-bound movements. Swing traders should identify the prevailing market conditions and select strategies that align with the current environment. Flexibility in strategy selection ensures that swing traders can capitalize on market opportunities while mitigating risks.

Position Trading Strategies

Position trading is a strategy that focuses on capturing long-term trends in the cryptocurrency market. Position traders hold positions for a long time, ranging from weeks to months or even years, compared to day traders or swing traders. This section explores the fundamentals of position trading in cryptocurrency markets, including its advantages, key strategies, risk management techniques, and the importance of patience and discipline.

Position trading is a long-term approach that aims to capitalize on significant price movements over an extended period. Position traders identify trends and enter positions aligned with the overall market direction. The objective is to capture most of a trend's upward or downward movement, maximizing profit potential.

Position trading allows traders to benefit from long-term trends in the cryptocurrency market. Holding positions for extended periods allows traders to ride substantial price movements and generate significant profits. This strategy takes advantage of the inherent volatility and growth potential in the cryptocurrency space.

Position trading requires less time commitment than day trading or swing trading. Traders can monitor their positions periodically rather than constantly tracking the market. This makes position trading suitable for individuals with busy schedules or those seeking a more passive approach to trading.

Position trading involves fewer trades and less frequent decision-making, reducing stress and emotional impact. Traders can avoid the constant pressure of making rapid decisions, allowing for a more relaxed and patient trading experience.

Position traders employ trend-following strategies to identify and capitalize on long-term market trends. They use technical analysis tools, such as moving averages, trend lines, and indicators like the Average Directional Index (ADX), to identify the prevailing trend. Position traders enter positions in the direction of the trend and hold them until the trend shows signs of reversal.

Position traders also consider fundamental factors when selecting cryptocurrencies for long-term positions. They assess the project's technology, team, adoption potential, and market positioning. By conducting thorough research, position traders aim to identify cryptocurrencies with strong fundamentals that have the potential for long-term growth.

Position traders diversify their cryptocurrency holdings to spread risk and capture opportunities across different projects. By allocating their capital across various cryptocurrencies, they mitigate the impact of individual project-specific risks. Diversification helps position traders build a robust portfolio that can weather market fluctuations and deliver superior returns.

Position traders allocate a portion of their trading capital to each position, ensuring that potential losses are within an acceptable risk tolerance level. By carefully managing position sizes, traders can protect their overall portfolio from significant drawdowns and limit exposure to any single cryptocurrency.

Position traders set long-term stop-loss orders to protect their positions from excessive losses. These orders are typically placed below key support levels or at predetermined percentage declines from the entry price. Long-term stop-loss orders provide a safety net and help manage risk during extended holding periods.

Patience and discipline are crucial qualities for successful position traders. They understand that trends take time to unfold and avoid the temptation to exit positions prematurely due to short-term market fluctuations. Position traders maintain a long-term perspective, allowing their positions to capture the full potential of the identified trend.

Position trading requires patience and continuous monitoring of positions. Traders must exercise discipline in sticking to their trading plan and resist the urge to make impulsive decisions based on short-term market fluctuations. Regular monitoring helps position traders assess the ongoing viability of their positions and make necessary adjustments if market conditions or project fundamentals change.

CHAPTER VI
Risk Management in Cryptocurrency Trading

Setting Risk Tolerance and Goals

Cryptocurrency trading offers exciting opportunities for investors to participate in the dynamic digital asset market. However, navigating this volatile landscape requires careful consideration of risk tolerance and the establishment of clear trading goals. In this section, we will explore the importance of setting risk tolerance and goals in cryptocurrency trading, the factors to consider when defining risk tolerance, strategies for goal setting, and the role of continuous assessment and adjustment.

Risk tolerance refers to an individual's willingness and ability to endure potential losses in pursuit of investment returns. Risk tolerance is crucial in crafting a trading strategy that aligns with one's financial goals and psychological comfort level. Understanding and defining risk tolerance is paramount when it comes to cryptocurrency trading, which can experience significant price fluctuations.

Evaluating one's financial position, including income, savings, and overall investment portfolio, is essential in determining risk tolerance. Traders should consider how much capital they are willing to allocate to cryptocurrency trading without jeopardizing their financial stability.

Experience in trading or investing, particularly in the cryptocurrency market, plays a role in assessing risk tolerance. Seasoned traders may have a higher risk tolerance due to their familiarity with market dynamics, while beginners may lean towards a more conservative approach.

Time horizon refers to the intended duration of the investment. Traders with longer investment horizons may have a higher risk tolerance as they have more time to recover from potential losses. Short-term traders or those with immediate financial needs may opt for a lower risk tolerance.

Traders should establish clear financial goals that align with their overall investment objectives. These goals may include generating a specific percentage of returns, achieving a certain profit target, or building a cryptocurrency portfolio of a specific value. Setting achievable and measurable financial goals provides a roadmap for trading decisions.

Goals should consider the desired risk-return balance. Traders should determine the level of risk they are comfortable taking in pursuit of their financial goals. Higher-risk strategies may offer the potential for greater returns but come with increased volatility, while lower-risk approaches may provide stability but with potentially lower returns.

Traders can set both long-term and short-term goals to guide their trading activities. Long-term goals may focus on wealth accumulation or retirement planning, while short-term goals may be oriented towards specific trading opportunities or achieving incremental growth.

Traders should regularly review their risk tolerance and trading goals to ensure they remain aligned with their evolving circumstances and market conditions. Changes in financial situation, market volatility, or personal circumstances may warrant risk tolerance and goal adjustments.

Rebalancing involves adjusting the portfolio's asset allocation based on performance and risk considerations. Traders can periodically assess their cryptocurrency holdings and make necessary adjustments to realign with their risk tolerance and goals.

Continuous learning and adaptation are integral to successful cryptocurrency trading. Traders should stay informed about market trends, new developments, and evolving regulatory landscapes. By staying abreast of industry knowledge, traders can make informed decisions and adjust their risk tolerance and goals accordingly.

Cryptocurrency trading can evoke strong emotions, such as fear and greed, which can impact decision-making. Traders should be aware of their emotional responses and cultivate emotional discipline. Maintaining a rational and disciplined approach to trading helps avoid impulsive actions and supports adherence to predetermined risk tolerance and goals.

Portfolio Diversification

Cryptocurrency trading offers a unique and dynamic investment opportunity but also comes with inherent risks due to market volatility. Portfolio diversification is a crucial strategy that can help traders mitigate risk and maximize returns. In this section, we will explore the importance of portfolio diversification in cryptocurrency trading, its benefits, key diversification strategies, and the role of ongoing monitoring and rebalancing.

Portfolio diversification involves spreading investments across different asset classes, sectors, and cryptocurrencies to reduce exposure to any single investment. By diversifying their portfolios, traders aim to achieve a balance between risk and potential returns. In cryptocurrency trading, portfolio diversification can help protect against the volatility and uncertainties associated with individual cryptocurrencies.

Diversifying a cryptocurrency portfolio helps reduce the impact of negative price movements on individual assets. By holding a mix of cryptocurrencies with different risk profiles and market correlations, traders can hedge against losses in any single investment.

Diversification can also enhance potential returns. While some cryptocurrencies may experience downturns, others may outperform the market. By having exposure to multiple cryptocurrencies, traders increase their chances of benefiting from the growth of successful projects.

Diversification helps preserve capital by minimizing the risk of catastrophic losses. Even if one cryptocurrency underperforms, the overall impact on the portfolio is reduced, allowing traders to preserve their trading capital and participate in future opportunities.

Traders should consider diversifying across different asset classes, including cryptocurrencies with varying risk profiles. Allocating a portion of the portfolio to established cryptocurrencies with lower volatility, such as Bitcoin or Ethereum, can provide stability. Additionally, including smaller-cap cryptocurrencies or emerging projects with higher growth potential adds a level of diversification to capture additional returns.

Investing in cryptocurrency from various industries can help traders diversify their portfolios. Different sectors, such as decentralized finance (DeFi), non-fungible tokens (NFTs), or blockchain interoperability, may experience varying levels of growth and volatility. By spreading investments across sectors, traders reduce exposure to sector-specific risks.

Geographical diversification involves investing in cryptocurrencies from different regions. Different countries and regions may have unique regulatory environments, market dynamics, and adoption rates. By diversifying across geographical regions, traders can mitigate the risk of concentration in a single jurisdiction.

Traders should regularly evaluate their cryptocurrency holdings and assess their performance, risk profiles, and market conditions. Monitoring market trends, news, and technological advancements helps identify opportunities and potential risks.

Rebalancing involves periodically adjusting the portfolio's allocation to maintain the desired diversification. Traders may rebalance their portfolios based on predefined criteria, such as target asset allocation percentages or market conditions. Rebalancing ensures that the portfolio remains aligned with the desired risk-return profile.

As cryptocurrency markets evolve, traders should consider adding promising new projects or removing underperforming assets from their portfolios. This active management helps capture emerging trends and reduces exposure to cryptocurrencies that no longer meet the desired criteria.

Traders should evaluate the risks associated with each cryptocurrency in their portfolio. Understanding factors such as project fundamentals, regulatory landscape, liquidity, and market sentiment helps assess the risk level of individual investments.

Traders should allocate capital to different cryptocurrencies based on their risk tolerance and the portfolio's overall risk profile. Proper position sizing ensures that no single investment dominates the portfolio's performance and mitigates the impact of potential losses.

While diversification is crucial, it's essential to strike a balance and avoid over-diversification. Holding too many cryptocurrencies may dilute potential returns and make staying informed about each investment challenging. Traders should aim for a manageable number of well-researched and carefully selected assets.

Stop-loss Orders and Risk Mitigation

Cryptocurrency trading offers lucrative opportunities but comes with inherent risks due to the market's volatility. Stop-loss orders are a vital risk management technique that can assist traders in properly protecting their capital. In this section, we will explore the importance of stop-loss orders in cryptocurrency trading, their benefits, key strategies for setting stop-loss levels, and the role of risk mitigation in achieving trading success.

A stop-loss order is a predefined order that automatically sells a cryptocurrency position when the price reaches a specific level, known as the stop price. Traders use stop-loss orders to limit potential losses and protect capital if the market moves against their positions. Stop-loss orders play a vital role in risk management and ensure traders can exit losing trades in a timely and controlled manner.

Stop-loss orders protect trading capital by limiting potential losses. By defining a predetermined exit point, traders can prevent losses from exceeding a predefined threshold. This helps safeguard their capital and ensures that a single trade does not have a disproportionately negative impact on their overall portfolio.

Stop-loss orders help traders overcome emotional biases that can cloud judgment during market fluctuations. By automating the exit process, traders remove the emotional component of decision-making and rely on a predetermined strategy. This helps traders stick to their risk management plan and avoid impulsive and irrational decisions based on fear or greed.

Stop-loss orders are an effective risk mitigation tool. They allow traders to limit potential losses in case of unexpected market events, sudden price drops, or adverse price movements. By implementing stop-loss orders, traders can define their risk tolerance and protect themselves from excessive downside risk.

One common approach is to set stop-loss levels based on a percentage of the entry price. Traders determine a tolerable percentage loss they are willing to accept and calculate the corresponding stop-loss level. For example, if a trader sets a 5% stop-loss, the order will trigger if the price falls 5% below the entry price.

Traders can set stop-loss levels based on key support levels, trend lines, or technical indicators. By identifying critical support and resistance levels, traders place stop-loss orders slightly below key levels to protect against significant price drops. This approach aligns with technical analysis strategies and helps traders exit positions if the market invalidates their anticipated price movement.

Volatility-based stop-loss orders consider the average volatility of a cryptocurrency to determine the appropriate stop-loss level. Traders analyze historical price movements and set stop-loss levels that account for expected price swings. This approach adapts to the inherent volatility of cryptocurrencies and helps protect against sharp price fluctuations.

Trailing stops are stop-loss orders that adjust dynamically as the price moves in the trader's favor. When the price increases, the trailing stop order moves up, maintaining a specific distance from the current market price. This allows traders to capture profits while still protecting against potential reversals.

Scaling out involves gradually reducing position sizes and adjusting stop-loss orders as the trade moves in favor of the trader. Traders lock in gains by taking partial profits and tightening stop-loss levels while maintaining exposure to potential further price movements. Scaling out helps traders manage risk and secure profits during extended price runs.

Effective risk management starts with proper position sizing. Traders should allocate a portion of their trading capital to each trade, considering their overall risk tolerance and the potential loss associated with the stop-loss level. By sizing positions appropriately, traders limit the impact of any single trade on their portfolio.

While stop-loss orders provide protection, it is essential to have contingency plans for extreme market scenarios. Traders should consider scenarios where stop-loss orders may not execute as expected due to liquidity issues or sudden market gaps. Having contingency plans in place ensures that traders are prepared to react and mitigate risks effectively.

Traders should monitor their positions and the overall market to identify potential changes in market conditions, project fundamentals, or regulatory developments. Continuous monitoring helps identify signals that may necessitate adjusting stop-loss levels or taking other risk management actions.

Emotion Control and Psychology of Trading

Trading in financial markets is a dynamic and complex endeavor that requires a deep understanding of market dynamics and the ability to control emotions and make rational decisions under pressure. The field of behavioral finance recognizes the significant role that emotions and psychology play in trading outcomes. This section will explore the importance of emotion control and the psychology of trading, examine common emotions that impact traders, discuss strategies for managing emotions, and highlight the key psychological factors contributing to successful trading.

Emotions can have a profound impact on trading decisions and outcomes. The two primary emotions that significantly influence traders are fear and greed. These emotions can cloud judgment, distort perception, and lead to irrational decision-making.

Humans naturally experience fear in the presence of danger or risk. Fear often arises when faced with potential market losses or uncertainty in trading. It can cause traders to exit positions prematurely, miss out on profitable opportunities, or avoid taking necessary risks. Fear can result in a defensive mindset that hinders the ability to make objective decisions based on market analysis and rational reasoning.

On the other hand, greed is an intense desire for more wealth or profit. It can manifest in traders' desire to maximize gains and often leads to taking excessive risks or holding on to losing positions in the hope of a turnaround. Greed can blind traders to the realities of the market, making them vulnerable to impulsive decisions and irrational behavior.

Managing emotions is crucial for successful trading. Here are some strategies to effectively manage emotions in trading:

The first step in managing emotions is to cultivate self-awareness. Traders must recognize their emotions and understand how they influence their decision-making process. This involves paying attention to thoughts, physical sensations, and behavioral patterns associated with different emotions. By becoming aware of their emotional states, traders can take steps to control and redirect their emotions effectively.

A well-defined trading plan acts as a roadmap for traders, providing structure and guidance during trading activities. It outlines specific entry and exit points, risk management strategies, and criteria for making trading decisions. Following a trading plan reduces emotional decision-making by providing a systematic approach to trading and removing impulsive actions driven by fear or greed.

Unrealistic expectations can fuel emotions such as greed or frustration. Traders should set realistic goals and understand that trading involves risks and uncertainties. By setting achievable expectations, traders can focus on the process rather than solely on the outcome. This helps manage emotions and reduces the psychological pressure associated with trading.

Effective risk management is crucial for emotional control. Traders should determine appropriate position sizing, set stop-loss orders to limit potential losses, and diversify their portfolios. By managing risk, traders can alleviate anxiety and fear, knowing that their overall exposure is controlled.

Discipline and patience are essential virtues in trading. Traders should stick to their trading plan, avoid impulsive actions, and exercise patience when waiting for favorable trading opportunities. Impulsive and emotionally driven decisions often lead to suboptimal outcomes. Traders can overcome emotional biases and make rational choices by practicing discipline and patience.

Beyond emotion control, several psychological factors contribute to successful trading. These factors are essential for traders to develop a strong mental framework and maintain a healthy trading mindset.

Trading involves inevitable ups and downs. The ability to recover from failures, setbacks, and periods of underperformance is known as mental resilience. Resilient traders understand that losses are part of the trading process and do not let them affect their confidence or decision-making abilities. They learn from their mistakes, adapt, and move forward with resilience.

Self-discipline is the ability to consistently adhere to a trading plan and follow predetermined rules. It involves controlling impulses, sticking to risk management strategies, and avoiding emotional decision-making. Self-discipline helps traders stay focused and maintain a disciplined approach to trading despite challenging market conditions.

Successful traders approach the market with an objective mindset. They base their decisions on thorough analysis, market research, and reliable indicators rather than emotional reactions or speculative impulses. Objectivity allows traders to make rational decisions based on facts and data rather than subjective biases.

The trading landscape constantly evolves, and successful traders recognize the importance of continuous learning and adaptation. They stay informed about market trends, economic indicators, and news that may impact their trades. Trading professionals may improve their methods, adjust to shifting market conditions, and remain on top of trends by engaging in continuous learning.

CHAPTER
VII
Advanced Trading Techniques

Margin Trading and Leveraged Positions

Margin trading and leveraged positions are advanced trading strategies that allow traders to amplify their potential profits and losses by borrowing funds from a broker. While these strategies can be lucrative, they also carry significant risks. In this section, we will explore the concept of margin trading, discuss how leverage works, examine the benefits and drawbacks of these strategies, delve into risk management techniques, and provide practical insights for successful margin trading.

Margin trading entails borrowing funds from a broker to trade assets with a higher value than the trader's initial capital. It allows traders to take larger positions in the market, potentially increasing their profits. The borrowed funds, known as the margin, act as collateral for the borrowed amount.

Traders must create a margin account with a brokerage that provides these services in order to engage in margin trading. The broker typically requires traders to deposit a certain percentage of the trade's value, known as the initial margin. This initial margin serves as a safeguard for the broker against potential losses.

The ratio of funds borrowed to the trader's own capital is known as leverage. It amplifies both potential gains and losses. For example, if a trader uses 1:10 leverage, they can control a position worth ten times their initial capital. While this magnifies potential profits, it also increases the exposure to potential losses.

Leverage can vary depending on the asset class and the broker's policies. Higher leverage ratios offer the potential for greater returns but also carry higher risks. Traders must carefully consider the leverage ratio they choose and understand its implications.

Margin trading allows traders to gain exposure to larger positions with limited capital. Traders can maximize their gains if the market moves in their favor by leveraging their investments.

Margin trading opens up opportunities in various markets that might otherwise be inaccessible due to capital limitations. Traders can explore different asset classes and markets to diversify their portfolios and exploit emerging trends.

Margin trading can contribute to overall market liquidity by allowing traders to participate in larger transactions. Increased liquidity can lead to more efficient markets and potentially narrower bid-ask spreads.

The main drawback of margin trading is the amplification of losses. If a trade moves against a leveraged position, the losses can exceed the trader's initial capital. To reduce possible losses, traders must carefully evaluate their risk tolerance and put risk management strategies into practice.

Margin trading involves continuous monitoring of positions. If the value of the leveraged position declines to a certain level, the broker may issue a margin call, requiring the trader to add more funds to meet the margin requirements. Failure to do so may result in forced liquidation of the position, potentially incurring significant losses.

Traders must establish clear risk parameters before engaging in margin trading. This includes determining the maximum amount of capital to allocate to margin trades, setting stop-loss orders to limit potential losses, and defining the acceptable level of leverage based on risk appetite and market conditions.

Margin traders should conduct comprehensive market analysis to make informed trading decisions. This includes analyzing technical indicators, studying market trends, and considering fundamental factors that may affect the asset's price. Thorough analysis helps traders identify favorable trade opportunities and minimize risks.

Continuous monitoring of leveraged positions is crucial in margin trading. Traders should keep a close eye on market conditions and the margin requirements set by the broker. Regular monitoring helps traders stay aware of potential risks and take timely action if needed.

Stop-loss orders are essential risk management tools in margin trading. They allow traders to automatically exit a position if the price reaches a predetermined level, limiting potential losses. Traders should set stop-loss orders based on their risk tolerance and incorporate them into their trading strategies.

Before engaging in margin trading, traders should invest time learning about these strategies' intricacies. They should understand the concept of leverage, margin requirements, risk management techniques, and the specific rules and policies of the broker they choose.

It is prudent for novice traders to start with smaller positions and lower leverage ratios. This allows them to gain experience and confidence in margin trading while limiting potential losses.

Margin trading should be part of a well-diversified portfolio. Traders should allocate their capital across different asset classes and employ risk management techniques, such as asset allocation and position sizing, to manage overall portfolio risk.

Traders should regularly assess their risk exposure and the performance of their margin trades. This involves analyzing the profitability of trades, reviewing risk management strategies, and adjusting trading plans as needed.

Arbitrage Trading Strategies

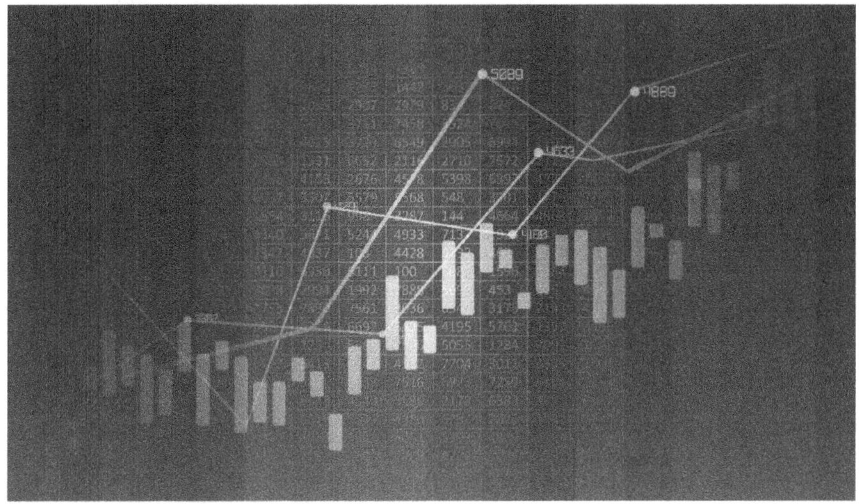

Trading strategies such as arbitrage can help investors profit from discrepancies in the price of the same or similar assets on other exchanges or markets. By taking advantage of these temporary market inefficiencies, traders aim to generate risk-free profits. In this section, we will explore the concept of arbitrage trading, discuss various types of arbitrage strategies, examine the benefits and challenges associated with arbitrage, and provide practical insights for successful arbitrage trading.

Arbitrage is the process of exploiting price differentials of the same asset in different markets. This strategy relies on the principle of the law of one price, which states that identical assets should have the same value regardless of their location or exchange.

Arbitrageurs attempt to profit from price discrepancies by simultaneously purchasing and selling the same asset in other marketplaces in order to take advantage of the price difference. The goal is to eliminate any risk and generate a guaranteed profit.

Spatial arbitrage involves exploiting price differences of the same asset in different geographical locations. Traders identify assets trading at different prices across other regions and take advantage of the price disparity by buying the asset in the lower-priced market and selling it in the higher-priced market.

Temporal arbitrage focuses on exploiting price differences of the same asset at different points in time. Traders identify assets that have experienced price discrepancies over time and capitalize on these variations. They make profit from the price difference by purchasing an asset at a cheap price and selling it at a higher price.

Statistical arbitrage involves using quantitative models and statistical analysis to identify pricing anomalies in the market. Traders create models that analyze historical data, correlations, and patterns to identify mispriced assets. They then execute trades based on the model's predictions, aiming to profit from the convergence of prices back to their fair value.

One of the key benefits of arbitrage trading is the potential for risk-free profits. By capitalizing on price discrepancies, traders can lock in profits without being exposed to market risk. This makes arbitrage an attractive strategy for risk-averse traders.

Arbitrage trading contributes to market efficiency by eliminating price discrepancies and ensuring the fair valuation of assets. The activity of arbitrageurs helps align prices across different markets, leading to more efficient pricing mechanisms.

The rise of advanced trading platforms and high-frequency trading has facilitated the execution of arbitrage strategies. Fast and efficient trading systems enable traders to identify and act upon price discrepancies in real time, enhancing the effectiveness of arbitrage trading.

Arbitrage trading has challenges. The speed and efficiency of execution are critical factors in successful arbitrage. Traders must have access to real-time market data, robust trading infrastructure, and fast execution capabilities to capitalize on fleeting price differentials.

As markets have become more efficient, genuine arbitrage opportunities have become rarer. The competition among arbitrageurs has increased, leading to narrower spreads and reduced profit margins. Traders need to continuously scan the markets and adapt their strategies to identify viable arbitrage opportunities.

Successful arbitrage trading requires in-depth research and analysis. Traders must monitor multiple markets, exchanges, and assets to identify price discrepancies. Advanced analytical tools and algorithms can assist in identifying potential arbitrage opportunities.

Although arbitrage trading is generally considered low-risk, it is essential to implement risk management strategies. Traders should set clear risk parameters, including position sizing, stop-loss orders, and diversification. Risk management helps protect against unexpected events and minimizes potential losses.

Speed and efficiency are crucial in arbitrage trading. Traders must have access to robust trading platforms, reliable market data, and fast execution capabilities. Implementing advanced trading technologies and utilizing co-location services can reduce latency and improve execution efficiency.

Arbitrage opportunities can emerge and disappear rapidly. Traders must continuously monitor markets, track prices, and adjust their strategies accordingly. Automated monitoring systems and alerts can assist in identifying and capitalizing on short-lived opportunities.

Algorithmic Trading and Trading Bots

Algorithmic trading and trading bots have revolutionized the financial markets, allowing traders to execute trades with unprecedented speed and efficiency. This section explores the concept of algorithmic trading, discusses the benefits and challenges associated with this approach, examines the role of trading bots, and provides practical insights for the successful implementation of algorithmic trading strategies.

Algorithmic trading, or algo trading, uses computer algorithms to automate trading decisions and execute orders in financial markets. These algorithms analyze market data, identify patterns, and make trading decisions based on pre-defined rules and strategies. Algorithmic trading relies on speed, accuracy, and the ability to process vast amounts of data in real-time.

The algorithms used in algorithmic trading can be based on various methodologies, including technical analysis, statistical models, machine learning, or a combination of these approaches. Traders program these algorithms to execute trades automatically, eliminating human intervention and emotions from trading.

Algorithmic trading allows traders to execute trades at a speed and frequency that would be impossible for human traders. Algorithms can analyze market data and make trading decisions in milliseconds, enabling traders to capitalize on fleeting market opportunities and react quickly to changing market conditions.

Algorithmic trading eliminates the potential for human error in trading decisions. The algorithms follow pre-defined rules and execute trades based on objective criteria, reducing the impact of emotions and cognitive biases. This results in more disciplined and consistent trading strategies.

Algorithms can automatically split large orders into smaller, manageable sizes and execute them across multiple exchanges or venues. This helps traders achieve better trade execution by accessing liquidity from various sources and minimizing market impact.

Algorithmic trading allows traders to backtest their strategies using historical market data. By simulating trades and evaluating performance, traders can optimize their algorithms to improve profitability and risk management. Backtesting helps traders gain confidence in their strategies before deploying them in live trading.

Algorithmic trading enables traders to diversify their portfolios across different assets, markets, and strategies. Automated execution allows traders to handle larger trade volumes and manage multiple positions simultaneously, scaling their trading activities more efficiently.

Algorithmic trading relies on robust, high-speed trading infrastructure, including low-latency connectivity, reliable data feeds, and advanced execution systems. Traders must invest in technology and maintain a stable and secure trading environment.

While algorithmic trading can be highly profitable, it is not immune to risks. Rapid market fluctuations, system failures, and unforeseen events can impact algorithmic strategies. Traders must carefully manage risk and implement safeguards to protect against potential losses.

Developing effective algorithmic trading strategies requires quantitative analysis, coding, and financial market expertise. Traders must continuously monitor and adapt their algorithms to changing market conditions, ensuring the strategies remain relevant and profitable.

Algorithmic trading is subject to regulatory requirements and compliance obligations. Traders must adhere to market rules and regulations governing algorithmic trading activities, including risk controls, reporting, and monitoring obligations.

Trading bots are computer programs that carry out trades automatically in accordance with pre-established rules and algorithms. These bots can be designed to operate in various market conditions, ranging from simple rule-based strategies to sophisticated machine-learning algorithms. Trading bots offer several advantages:

Trading bots can monitor the market 24/7, scanning for trading opportunities and executing trades without human intervention. This eliminates the need for traders to monitor the market manually constantly.

Bots can execute trades at high speed, leveraging algorithmic strategies to capitalize on market inefficiencies. As a result, traders may execute trades quickly and profit from short-term price changes.

Trading bots operate based on pre-defined rules and algorithms, removing emotional biases from the trading process. This leads to more disciplined and consistent trading decisions.

The performance and strategy of bots can be evaluated using historical data through backtesting. This helps traders refine their algorithms and improve their profitability.

Traders should thoroughly research and develop their algorithmic trading strategies. They must understand the underlying principles, select appropriate methodologies, and define clear rules and risk parameters. Testing and refining the strategies before deploying them in live trading is crucial.

Traders must invest in a reliable, high-speed trading infrastructure to support algorithmic trading activities. This includes low-latency connectivity, stable data feeds, and efficient execution systems. Redundancy measures should be in place to minimize downtime and system failures.

Effective risk management is essential in algorithmic trading. Traders should implement risk controls, such as position sizing, stop-loss orders, and portfolio diversification. Regular monitoring and evaluating performance metrics are crucial for identifying and managing risks.

Traders must adhere to regulatory requirements and compliance obligations associated with algorithmic trading. They should stay updated on regulatory changes and ensure their trading activities align with the applicable rules and guidelines.

Social Trading and Copy Trading

As innovative approaches in the financial markets, social trading and copy trading enable traders to gain from the accumulated knowledge of a community. These platforms enable traders to connect, share insights, and replicate the trades of successful traders. In this section, we will explore the concept of social trading and copy trading, discuss their benefits and challenges, examine the role of technology in enabling these practices, and provide practical insights for successful participation in these platforms.

Social trading involves sharing trading ideas, strategies, and insights among a community of traders. It allows traders to interact with each other, follow the trades of successful individuals, and discuss market trends and opportunities. Social trading platforms facilitate this exchange of information and enable traders to learn from each other's experiences.

On the other hand, copy trading is a subset of social trading that automatically allows traders to replicate successful traders' trades. In copy trading platforms, traders can choose to allocate a portion of their capital to mimic the trades executed by selected traders. The trades are replicated in real-time, allowing traders to benefit from the expertise and performance of others.

Social trading platforms provide a unique learning environment where traders can interact with experienced individuals. Novice traders can gain insights into market trends, strategies, and risk management techniques from seasoned traders. This knowledge-sharing fosters a collaborative learning environment that can accelerate a trader's learning curve.

Social trading platforms give traders access to various experts and successful traders. By following and replicating the trades of these individuals, traders can tap into the expertise and strategies of seasoned professionals. This access to expert insights can be particularly valuable for traders who are new to the markets or looking to diversify their trading approaches.

Copy trading eliminates the need for traders to conduct extensive research and analysis independently. Market research, trade execution, and monitoring may all be done more quickly and efficiently by copying the trades of successful traders. This time efficiency allows traders to focus on other aspects of their trading strategies or engage in additional learning opportunities.

Social trading and copy trading allow traders to diversify their portfolios by following multiple traders with different trading styles and strategies. Diversification can spread risk and reduce the impact of a single trader's performance on the overall portfolio. By copying trades from various successful traders, traders can achieve a balanced and diversified trading approach.

Copy trading removes emotional biases from the trading process. Traders can avoid making impulsive decisions driven by fear or greed by relying on the trading decisions of successful traders. Copying trades based on pre-defined rules and strategies helps maintain discipline and objectivity in the trading process.

While social and copy trading offer benefits, they also come with inherent risks. Traders must carefully manage their risk exposure and consider factors such as the performance history, risk tolerance, and trading style of the traders they choose to copy. Setting appropriate risk parameters and allocating capital wisely to mitigate potential losses is crucial.

The success of social trading and copy trading relies on the transparency and accuracy of the information provided by the traders being followed. Traders must ensure that the performance data, trading history, and risk metrics of the traders they follow are accurate and reliable. Verification processes and reputation systems implemented by social trading platforms play a crucial role in establishing trust among traders.

Copying trades in real-time means that traders are exposed to the same market conditions and potential price fluctuations as the traders they follow. Market volatility and timing can significantly impact the outcomes of copied trades. Traders should be aware of these factors and carefully consider the potential risks associated with replicating trades during volatile market periods.

Copy trading can lead to an overreliance on the performance of others. Traders must remember that past performance is not necessarily indicative of future results. It is essential to conduct independent research and analysis, understand the strategies being copied, and continuously evaluate the traders' performance.

The rapid advancement of technology has been instrumental in the growth and popularity of social trading and copy trading platforms. These platforms leverage sophisticated algorithms, data analytics, and user-friendly interfaces to facilitate seamless interaction and replication of trades.

Social trading platforms provide a range of features that enhance the user experience. These features include real-time trade copying, performance statistics, risk metrics, and communication tools for traders to share insights and interact. User-friendly interfaces make it easy for traders to find and follow successful traders and access the relevant information needed for informed decision-making.

Social trading platforms analyze vast amounts of data to identify successful traders, evaluate performance, and generate insights. These platforms employ advanced algorithms and statistical models to track trading patterns, risk-adjusted returns, and other key metrics. Data analysis helps traders identify traders with consistent performance and refine their own trading strategies.

Social trading platforms often provide risk management tools that allow traders to set stop-loss orders, allocate capital, and define risk parameters. These tools help traders manage risk effectively and protect their capital. Integrating risk management tools within the platforms ensures that traders can implement appropriate risk controls when copying trades.

When choosing traders to follow or copy, traders should consider factors such as historical performance, risk metrics, trading style, and market expertise. It is crucial to assess the consistency and reliability of a trader's performance over time, rather than solely focusing on short-term gains. Diversifying the selection of traders can also help mitigate risk and achieve a balanced portfolio.

Traders should regularly monitor the performance of the traders they follow or copy. It is crucial to assess whether the copied trades align with one's own trading goals and risk tolerance. Constant evaluation helps identify underperforming traders and make necessary adjustments to the copied portfolio.

While copy trading can save time and effort, traders should only partially detach themselves from the trading process. Active involvement in the markets, conducting independent research, and staying updated on market trends are essential for understanding the context and risks associated with copying trades.

Effective risk management is critical in social trading and copy trading. Traders should set appropriate risk parameters, allocate capital wisely, and diversify their copied trade portfolios. Risk controls, such as stop-loss orders, can help limit potential losses and protect capital.

CHAPTER VIII
Evaluating and Selecting Cryptocurrencies

Researching and Analyzing Cryptocurrencies

Cryptocurrencies have revolutionized the financial landscape, offering decentralized and borderless digital assets with the potential for financial independence and innovation. It is more important for traders and investors to have efficient research and analysis methods as the popularity of cryptocurrencies rises. This section delves into the world of researching and analyzing cryptocurrencies, discussing the fundamental factors, technical analysis, and market indicators that can help make informed investment decisions.

Researching and analyzing cryptocurrencies involves comprehensively examining various aspects of a specific digital asset. This process goes beyond simply looking at the price and market trends; it encompasses a deep understanding of the underlying technology, the project's fundamentals, market dynamics, and investor sentiment. Investors can acquire important insights into the potential value and future prospects of a cryptocurrency by undertaking thorough research and analysis.

Fundamental analysis starts with understanding the technology behind a cryptocurrency and its real-world use case. Evaluating the underlying blockchain technology, consensus mechanisms, scalability, and security features can help assess a cryptocurrency's long-term viability and potential adoption.

A cryptocurrency project's success is greatly influenced by the team working on it. Researching the development team's experience, credentials, and track record can provide insights into their ability to execute the project's goals. Additionally, assessing the size and engagement of the community surrounding a cryptocurrency can gauge its level of support and potential for growth.

Partnerships with established companies and institutions can boost the credibility and adoption of a cryptocurrency. Analyzing the strategic alliances and collaborations can provide insights into the cryptocurrency's potential market reach and integration within existing ecosystems.

Understanding the competitive landscape of a cryptocurrency is essential. Analyzing competing projects, their features, and market positioning can help assess the unique value proposition of a cryptocurrency and its potential for market adoption.

Technical analysis involves studying historical price data and identifying trends, patterns, and chart formations. This analysis helps identify support and resistance levels, trendlines, and potential price reversals. By examining price movements, traders can make predictions about future price behavior.

Technical indicators and oscillators provide additional insights into market trends and momentum. These tools, such as moving averages, relative strength index (RSI), and stochastic oscillators, help identify overbought or oversold conditions and potential trend reversals.

Analyzing trading volume is crucial in technical analysis. Volume provides insights into market participation and the strength of price movements. High volume during price increases or decreases can confirm the validity of a trend, while low volume may indicate a lack of market interest or potential trend reversal.

Candlestick patterns offer valuable information about market sentiment and potential price reversals. Patterns like doji, hammer, and engulfing patterns provide insights into shifts in supply and demand dynamics.

Market capitalization is a key indicator of a cryptocurrency's size and relative value in the market. It is determined by multiplying the current price by the total supply of tokens or coins. Market capitalization provides a snapshot of the cryptocurrency's overall worth and can be used for comparisons with other cryptocurrencies.

The total number of shares or tokens traded within a given time period is referred to as the trading volume. High trading volume indicates market liquidity and active participation, while low volume may indicate a lack of interest or reduced market activity.

Monitoring social media platforms and news outlets can provide insights into investor sentiment and market trends. Positive or negative sentiment expressed by the community or influential figures can impact the price and adoption of a cryptocurrency.

Regulatory developments and legal frameworks significantly impact the cryptocurrency market. Monitoring regulatory announcements and legal considerations can help assess the potential risks and challenges that a cryptocurrency may face.

Assessing the security of a cryptocurrency's underlying technology, including vulnerabilities and potential hacking risks, is essential. Additionally, understanding the level of decentralization and governance mechanisms can help evaluate the resilience of a cryptocurrency project.

Cryptocurrency markets are known for their volatility, which presents both opportunities and risks. Traders and investors must consider the potential for significant price fluctuations and implement risk management strategies such as stop-loss orders and proper position sizing.

Liquidity is vital in cryptocurrency trading. Thinly traded or illiquid markets can challenge executing trades at desired prices. Analyzing trading volumes, order books, and market depth can help assess the liquidity of a cryptocurrency and potential slippage risks.

Regulatory developments and legal uncertainties can impact the cryptocurrency market. Traders and investors should stay updated on regulatory changes and consider the potential legal implications and compliance requirements associated with a cryptocurrency.

Relying on multiple reputable sources for information and analysis helps avoid biases and provides a broader perspective. Combining various resources, such as cryptocurrency news websites, technical analysis platforms, and community forums, can offer a comprehensive understanding of a cryptocurrency.

Cryptocurrency markets are dynamic and ever-evolving. Staying updated on market trends, technological advancements, and regulatory developments is crucial for effective research and analysis. Engaging in online communities, attending industry conferences, and reading whitepapers can provide valuable insights.

Utilizing analytical tools and platforms designed explicitly for cryptocurrency research and analysis can streamline the process. These tools often provide access to historical data, charting capabilities, technical indicators, and sentiment analysis features.

Establishing a well-defined risk management strategy is vital in cryptocurrency investing and trading. Setting clear entry and exit points, implementing stop-loss orders, and diversifying the portfolio across different cryptocurrencies can help manage risk exposure effectively.

Assessing Tokenomics and Utility

In the world of cryptocurrencies, tokenomics refers to a cryptocurrency token's economic structure and design. Tokenomics encompasses various factors, including the token's utility, distribution, supply dynamics, governance mechanisms, and incentives. Assessing tokenomics is crucial for investors and participants in the cryptocurrency ecosystem, as it provides insights into a token's value proposition and potential long-term viability. This section explores the concept of tokenomics, delves into the assessment of token utility, and discusses the key considerations for evaluating the economic dynamics of cryptocurrency tokens.

Tokenomics refers to the economic framework of a cryptocurrency token. It involves studying how tokens are created, distributed, and utilized within a specific blockchain ecosystem. Tokenomics encompasses several elements that contribute to a token's overall value and utility.

Token distribution refers to the initial allocation of tokens and subsequent distribution over time. Examining the distribution model helps assess factors such as fairness, concentration of ownership, and potential impact on market dynamics.

The token supply and inflation rate play a significant role in tokenomics. Understanding the maximum supply of tokens, inflation mechanisms (if any), and potential token burn mechanisms provides insights into tokens' scarcity and future availability.

Governance mechanisms dictate how decisions are made within a blockchain ecosystem. Assessing the governance structure and the role of token holders in decision-making processes helps determine the level of decentralization, transparency, and community involvement.

Tokenomics often includes mechanisms to incentivize and reward token holders for their participation and contributions to the ecosystem. These incentives can include staking rewards, network participation rewards, or discounts on platform services. Evaluating the effectiveness of these incentives is crucial to understanding the potential value and adoption of a token.

Token utility refers to the functionality and purpose of a cryptocurrency token within its ecosystem. Understanding the utility of a token is essential for evaluating its potential value and long-term prospects. Several aspects contribute to token utility.

Many cryptocurrencies serve as a medium of exchange, allowing users to transact value within the ecosystem. Assessing the acceptance and adoption of a token as a means of payment or exchange is crucial to understanding its utility and potential for widespread use.

Some tokens provide access to specific platforms or services within a blockchain ecosystem. Evaluating the utility of a token in terms of accessing and utilizing platform features, such as decentralized applications (dApps) or smart contracts, helps gauge its value proposition.

Tokens often grant holders the right to participate in governance and decision-making processes within the ecosystem. Assessing the extent of voting rights and the influence of token holders can provide insights into the level of decentralization and community involvement.

It is essential to differentiate between utility tokens and security tokens. Utility tokens are designed to provide specific services or access to platforms, while security tokens represent ownership in an underlying asset or company. Understanding the distinction between these types of tokens is crucial for evaluating their utility and compliance with regulatory frameworks.

The success of a token heavily depends on market demand and adoption. Assessing the level of interest, user adoption, and partnerships within the ecosystem can provide insights into a token's potential growth and value appreciation.

Evaluating how well the tokenomics align with the project's goals and vision is crucial. A well-designed tokenomic structure should incentivize desired behaviors, promote ecosystem growth, and align participants' interests with the project's success.

Token burn mechanisms, where a portion of tokens is permanently removed from circulation, can positively impact token value by increasing scarcity. Assessing the token burn schedule, frequency, and potential impact on supply dynamics is important for understanding the long-term value proposition.

Compliance with regulatory frameworks is essential for the long-term viability of a token. Evaluating whether a token complies with relevant securities, financial, and consumer protection regulations is crucial for assessing its potential risks and legal implications.

To illustrate the assessment of tokenomics and utility, it is beneficial to examine real-world examples of successful tokens and their economic dynamics. Case studies such as Ethereum (ETH), Binance Coin (BNB), and Uniswap (UNI) can provide insights into how tokenomics and utility contribute to their success.

Ethereum's tokenomics include ETH as the native token used for transaction fees, smart contract execution, and as a medium of exchange within the Ethereum ecosystem. ETH's utility is fundamental to the functioning of the Ethereum blockchain, making it a critical component of the decentralized finance (DeFi) ecosystem.

Binance exchange native token, BNB, has a variety of uses. It can be used to pay for trading fees, participate in token sales on the Binance Launchpad, and access various services within the Binance ecosystem. BNB's utility and strong integration within the Binance platform have contributed to its adoption and value appreciation.

UNI is the governance token of the Uniswap decentralized exchange (DEX). UNI holders have voting rights and can participate in governance decisions related to protocol upgrades, fee structures, and platform development. The utility of UNI as a governance token aligns with Uniswap's decentralized ethos and community involvement.

Cryptocurrency markets are known for their volatility. The value of tokens can be considerably impacted by price changes, thus it is crucial to take into account the potential risks brought on by market volatility.

The regulatory landscape surrounding cryptocurrencies is constantly evolving. Assessing a token's potential regulatory risks and compliance requirements is crucial for understanding its long-term prospects.

Evaluating the technical robustness, security, and scalability of a blockchain platform supporting a token is essential. Understanding the risks associated with potential vulnerabilities, network congestion, or lack of adoption can provide insights into the token's viability.

Understanding Whitepapers and Roadmaps

Cryptocurrency trading requires a thorough understanding of the projects being invested in. Whitepapers and roadmaps play a vital role in this process by providing valuable insights into cryptocurrency projects' vision, technology, and development plans. This section will explore the significance of whitepapers and roadmaps, their role in cryptocurrency trading, and how they offer essential information to evaluate projects effectively.

Whitepapers serve as comprehensive documents that outline a cryptocurrency project's technical specifications, features, and goals. They aim to introduce the project to potential investors, developers, and the wider community. By delving into whitepapers, traders gain access to in-depth technical details, innovative technology explanations, and an understanding of the project's potential impact on the market. Whitepapers also provide insights into the market analysis and use cases that the project aims to address, giving traders a clearer picture of its target audience and value proposition.

Roadmaps, in contrast, offer a visual representation of the project's development milestones, timeline, and goals. They serve as strategic plans that outline the project's objectives and the necessary steps to achieve them. Roadmaps provide transparency and allow stakeholders to track the project's progress over time. By assessing a project's roadmap, traders can evaluate its adherence to the outlined timeline and assess its commitment to transparency and accountability. Roadmaps also enable traders to gain insights into the various development phases and milestones, such as the launch of the mainnet, the introduction of key features, partnerships, or expansion into new markets.

To effectively evaluate cryptocurrency projects, traders should consider several factors when analyzing whitepapers and roadmaps:

Whitepapers provide detailed technical information about the project's underlying technology, including blockchain architecture, consensus mechanisms, scalability solutions, and security features. Traders should assess the technical feasibility of the proposed solution and determine if it aligns with their expectations. Evaluating the technical aspects helps ascertain the project's potential for achieving its stated objectives.

Whitepapers often introduce the project's team members and advisors. Traders should carefully evaluate the team's expertise, industry experience, and track record. A competent and experienced team enhances the project's credibility and increases the likelihood of successful execution. Assessing the qualifications and background of the team members and advisors is crucial in determining the project's potential for success.

Whitepapers typically include a market analysis section that identifies the problem the project aims to solve and presents potential use cases. Traders should assess the size of the target market, the competitive landscape, and the project's unique value proposition. Understanding the market analysis helps determine if the project has identified a viable market niche and if it can effectively compete with existing solutions.

Traders should critically evaluate the project's roadmap for realism and achievability. It is essential to assess the progress made against the outlined milestones. Projects that consistently meet or exceed their development targets demonstrate higher reliability and execution capability. Evaluating the project's progress against the roadmap helps traders gauge the project's commitment to its stated goals and its ability to deliver on its promises.

Identifying Potential Investment Opportunities

Investing in cryptocurrencies has emerged as a lucrative opportunity in the modern financial landscape, offering potential high returns and diversification options. However, with thousands of cryptocurrencies available, identifying promising investment opportunities requires a systematic approach and thorough analysis. This section explores the process of identifying potential investment opportunities in the cryptocurrency market, delving into fundamental analysis, market research, risk assessment, and strategic decision-making.

Before delving into identifying investment opportunities, it is crucial to understand the cryptocurrency market and its dynamics. The cryptocurrency market is known for its volatility, liquidity, and the emergence of new projects. Key factors to consider include:

Market capitalization reflects the overall value of a cryptocurrency and is determined by multiplying the price of a token by its circulating supply. It indicates the size and relative worth of a cryptocurrency in the market.

Monitoring market trends, including price movements, trading volumes, and sentiment analysis, helps gauge the overall market sentiment and investor perception of cryptocurrencies.

The regulatory landscape surrounding cryptocurrencies varies globally. Understanding the regulatory environment and potential legal implications is crucial for assessing the risks and opportunities associated with specific cryptocurrencies.

Fundamental analysis is a critical component of identifying potential investment opportunities. It involves evaluating a cryptocurrency's intrinsic value and long-term prospects based on its underlying technology, use case, team, partnerships, and market competition. Key considerations include:

Assessing a cryptocurrency's technological innovation, scalability, security, and real-world use case is essential. Understanding its unique value proposition and the potential for mass adoption is crucial for long-term investment prospects.

The expertise, track record, and commitment of the project team play a vital role in the success of a cryptocurrency. Evaluating the team's experience, qualifications, and community engagement can provide insights into their ability to execute the project's goals.

Partnerships with established companies, institutions, or industry players can significantly impact the credibility and adoption of a cryptocurrency. Assessing strategic alliances and collaborations can help gauge the potential market reach and integration within existing ecosystems.

Analyzing the competitive landscape and distinguishing factors of a cryptocurrency is essential. Evaluating competing projects, their features, and market positioning can help identify unique value propositions and potential advantages.

Technical analysis complements fundamental analysis by studying historical price data, chart patterns, and market indicators. It helps identify trends, support and resistance levels, and potential entry and exit points for investment decisions. Key elements include:

Analyzing historical price data helps identify trends, chart patterns, and potential price reversals. Identifying support and resistance levels and understanding market dynamics assists in determining optimal entry and exit points.

Moving averages, stochastic oscillators, and relative strength index (RSI) are examples of technical indicators that offer various perspectives on market trends and momentum. These tools help identify overbought or oversold conditions and potential trend reversals.

Analyzing trading volume provides insights into market participation and the strength of price movements. High volume during price increases or decreases confirms the validity of a trend, while low volume may indicate a lack of market interest or potential trend reversal.

Monitoring social media platforms, news outlets, and online communities can provide insights into investor sentiment and market trends. The negative or positive sentiment expressed by the community or influential figures can impact the price and adoption of a cryptocurrency.

Identifying potential investment opportunities also requires assessing the associated risks and implementing risk mitigation strategies. Key considerations include:

The cryptocurrency market is known for its volatility. Evaluating the potential price fluctuations and implementing risk management strategies such as stop-loss orders and diversification helps manage risk exposure effectively.

Assessing the security vulnerabilities, regulatory compliance, and legal risks associated with a cryptocurrency is essential. Understanding potential risks and challenges related to hacking, scams, or regulation changes is crucial for informed decision-making.

Evaluating the project's viability, scalability, and execution capabilities is crucial. Assessing the progress and adherence to the project roadmap, development updates, and community involvement can provide insights into the project's potential for success.

Liquidity is necessary when considering investment opportunities. Thinly traded or illiquid markets can present challenges in executing trades at desired prices. Analyzing trading volumes, order books, and market depth helps assess the liquidity and potential slippage risks.

Identifying potential investment opportunities is only the first step. Implementing a strategic decision-making process and managing a well-diversified portfolio is crucial for long-term success. Key elements include:

Defining investment goals, such as short-term trading or long-term holding, helps determine the appropriate investment strategies and timeframes.

Spreading investments across different cryptocurrencies, asset classes, and risk levels reduces exposure to specific risks and increases the potential for returns. Diversification helps manage risk and optimize returns.

Assessing personal risk tolerance and aligning investment decisions with individual risk appetite is essential. Determining the appropriate position sizing based on risk tolerance helps manage potential losses and optimize returns.

The cryptocurrency market is dynamic and rapidly evolving. Continuous learning, staying updated on market trends, technological advancements, and regulatory changes, and adapting investment strategies are crucial for long-term success.

CHAPTER
IX
Staying Informed and Adapting
to Market Changes

News Sources and Cryptocurrency Communities

Cryptocurrency trading is a dynamic and ever-evolving field, and staying informed and connected is crucial for navigating the complexities of the market. News sources and cryptocurrency communities play a vital role in providing traders and enthusiasts with up-to-date information, market insights, and opportunities for collaboration. This section will explore the significance of news sources and cryptocurrency communities in the crypto space, highlighting their impact on market awareness, analysis, and community engagement.

In the fast-paced world of cryptocurrency trading, news sources dedicated to cryptocurrencies deliver real-time information on market developments, regulatory changes, and technological advancements. By staying updated with the latest news, traders can make timely decisions and adapt their strategies to changing market conditions. Reputable news sources also offer expert analysis and commentary, providing valuable insights into market trends, price movements, and potential investment opportunities. This in-depth analysis helps traders understand the underlying factors driving market dynamics and make informed trading decisions. Furthermore, news sources cover regulatory updates, government announcements, and legal developments, offering traders clarity on compliance requirements and potential impacts on the market. Lastly, with cryptocurrencies being driven by technological innovation, news sources cover emerging technologies, blockchain advancements, and decentralized finance (DeFi) developments, providing traders with valuable knowledge to identify promising projects and investment opportunities.

News sources in the cryptocurrency space can be categorized into various types. Established financial news outlets such as Bloomberg, Reuters, and CNBC now dedicate significant coverage to cryptocurrencies. These sources provide reliable information, analysis, and insights on both traditional finance and the crypto market. Additionally, specialized news platforms focus solely on cryptocurrencies and blockchain technology. Platforms like CoinDesk, Cointelegraph, and CryptoSlate provide in-depth coverage, expert opinions, and investigative journalism specific to the crypto industry. Social media platforms, particularly Twitter and Reddit, have also become essential sources of real-time news and community engagement. Cryptocurrency influencers, industry experts, and project teams often share news, analysis, and insights, creating a vibrant information exchange ecosystem.

Cryptocurrency communities are crucial in fostering collaboration, idea sharing, and knowledge exchange. Online forums like Bitcointalk and Reddit's cryptocurrency subreddits allow individuals to engage with like-minded enthusiasts, seek advice, and discuss market trends. Numerous cryptocurrency projects have dedicated communities where users can communicate with other investors and the development team in real time. These communities offer a deeper understanding of project goals, updates, and potential investment opportunities. Furthermore, cryptocurrency communities provide educational resources, tutorials, and support for newcomers. Engaging with experienced community members helps newcomers navigate the market's complexities and learn from others' experiences.

In the cryptocurrency space, it is crucial to verify the accuracy of news sources and exercise critical thinking skills. Cross-referencing information across multiple reputable sources and conducting independent research ensures the reliability of the news and helps avoid potential misinformation or rumors. Developing critical thinking skills allows traders to assess the credibility of sources, consider potential biases, and evaluate the evidence and supporting arguments presented. Seeking expert opinions can provide valuable insights, particularly in complex or uncertain situations. Engaging with reputable analysts, researchers, or financial advisors helps validate information and better understand market trends.

Tracking Market Sentiment

The world of cryptocurrency trading is not only driven by numbers and charts but also by the emotions and beliefs of market participants. Understanding market sentiment, which refers to the overall emotional attitude of traders and investors towards a particular asset or market, is crucial for making informed trading decisions. This section will explore the importance of tracking market sentiment in cryptocurrency trading, the various methods and tools available for sentiment analysis, and how traders can leverage this information to enhance their trading strategies and outcomes.

Market sentiment is significant in driving price movements and determining market trends. It reflects traders' and investors' collective emotions and beliefs, shaping their buying and selling decisions. Positive market sentiment often leads to increased buying activity, driving prices higher, while negative sentiment can trigger selling pressure and drive prices lower. By understanding and tracking market sentiment, traders can gain valuable insights into the prevailing market sentiment and anticipate potential price movements.

News articles, social media platforms, and online forums are valuable sources of information for sentiment analysis. By analyzing news sentiment and monitoring platforms like Twitter, Reddit, and Telegram, traders can gain a sense of public opinion and sentiment towards specific cryptocurrencies or the market as a whole. Natural language processing techniques and sentiment analysis tools can help process and interpret the vast amount of textual data available.

While technical indicators primarily focus on price and volume data, some indicators indirectly reflect market sentiment. For instance, Moving Average Convergence Divergence (MACD) and Relative Strength Index (RSI) might reveal overbought or oversold conditions and potential fluctuations in sentiment. Volume analysis can also offer clues about the strength of buying or selling pressure, which can reflect changes in sentiment.

Several market sentiment indexes aggregate data from multiple sources to provide an overall sentiment reading. These indexes consider factors such as social media mentions, news sentiment, and trading volume to gauge the sentiment of market participants. Examples include the Crypto Fear and Greed Index and the Crypto Volatility Index.

Contrarian traders use market sentiment as a contrarian indicator. They believe that the market is likely to reverse when sentiment becomes excessively positive or negative. For example, if market sentiment is overwhelmingly bullish, contrarian traders may take a cautious approach and consider selling or taking short positions.

Conversely, they may consider taking long positions when sentiment is overly bearish.

Market sentiment can act as a confirmation tool for existing trends. If sentiment aligns with a particular trend, it can provide additional confidence in the continuation of that trend. For instance, if sentiment is overwhelmingly bullish and supports an upward price trend, traders may consider adding to long positions or adjusting their take-profit levels.

Changes in market sentiment can serve as early warning signs of potential trend reversals or market shifts. Monitoring sentiment can help traders anticipate major price movements or identify periods of increased market volatility. By being aware of shifts in sentiment, traders can adjust their strategies accordingly and take protective measures to mitigate potential risks.

While tracking market sentiment can be valuable, it also comes with challenges and considerations. Sentiment analysis is subjective and influenced by individual biases. Additionally, sentiment indicators are not foolproof and can be affected by market manipulation or false signals. Traders should approach sentiment analysis with caution and consider it as one piece of the puzzle, integrating it with other technical and fundamental analysis tools to gain a comprehensive view of the market.

Adapting Strategies to Market Volatility

Volatility is an inherent characteristic of the cryptocurrency market, with price fluctuations that can be dramatic and rapid. Adapting strategies to market volatility is essential for traders and investors seeking to navigate the challenges and capitalize on the opportunities presented by price movements. This section explores the significance of market volatility, its impact on trading strategies, risk management techniques, and the importance of flexibility and adaptability in the dynamic cryptocurrency market.

The cryptocurrency market is known for its inherent volatility, which refers to the price variability in a financial market. In cryptocurrencies, market volatility can be attributed to various factors, including speculation, investor sentiment, market liquidity, regulatory developments, and market manipulation. Understanding market volatility is crucial as it influences trading strategies, risk management, and overall trading performance.

Market volatility profoundly impacts trading strategies, influencing decision-making, risk management, and overall trading performance. High market volatility presents increased trading opportunities but also comes with heightened risk. Traders must adapt their strategies to account for the impact of volatility on technical analysis indicators, emotional factors, and investor behavior.

Successful adaptation to market volatility requires implementing appropriate strategies and risk management techniques. Traders and investors can navigate the challenges and capitalize on opportunities by diversifying their portfolios, adjusting position sizes, utilizing stop-loss orders and trailing stops, employing volatility-based strategies, and being flexible with timeframes. These strategies help manage risk, optimize returns, and take advantage of price movements during periods of heightened volatility.

The cryptocurrency market is dynamic, and market conditions can change rapidly. Continuous learning and adaptation are vital for traders and investors seeking to adapt to market volatility effectively. It is essential to refine technical analysis skills continuously, stay updated on fundamental factors, assess risk tolerance, and regularly monitor market conditions. By embracing a mindset of continuous learning and adaptation, traders and investors can make informed decisions and optimize their strategies in response to changing market dynamics.

While market volatility poses challenges, it also presents unique opportunities for traders and investors. Volatile markets offer profit potential for those who can correctly anticipate price movements and implement effective trading strategies. Market inefficiencies can be exploited through arbitrage or taking advantage of price disparities across different exchanges. Moreover, periods of market volatility can be an opportunity to accumulate assets at favorable prices and capitalize on long-term growth potential.

Continuous Learning and Skill Development

The cryptocurrency market is a dynamic and rapidly evolving landscape that demands continuous learning and skill development. With technological advancements, regulatory changes, and market trends shaping the industry, staying ahead of the curve is essential for traders, investors, and enthusiasts. This section explores the significance of continuous learning and skill development in the cryptocurrency market, highlighting the benefits, strategies, and resources available to nurture success in this ever-changing ecosystem.

The constant process of picking up new information, abilities, and perspectives is known as continuous learning. In the cryptocurrency market, where innovation and disruption are constant, continuous learning is pivotal for several reasons. Firstly, in order to make wise decisions and stay ahead of the curve, it is first important to stay informed about industry trends. Secondly, continuous learning enables individuals to adapt to market dynamics and navigate technological changes, regulations, and market trends. Thirdly, it helps individuals navigate the complexity of the cryptocurrency market by understanding the underlying technologies and grasping economic and governance concepts. Lastly, continuous learning enhances decision-making skills, critical thinking abilities, and risk assessment capabilities, which are essential for success in the cryptocurrency market.

Developing a strategic approach to continuous learning in the cryptocurrency market is crucial. The following strategies can be employed to foster ongoing growth and skill development. Firstly, setting learning goals provides direction and motivation. These goals can include acquiring knowledge about specific cryptocurrencies, learning new technical analysis techniques, or understanding regulatory developments. Secondly, diversifying learning sources broadens perspectives and ensures a well-rounded education. Utilizing books, online courses, webinars, podcasts, industry conferences, and engaging with cryptocurrency communities contributes to continuous learning. Thirdly, following industry experts and influential figures within the cryptocurrency space provides valuable insights and exposure to their analyses and opinions. Fourthly, joining cryptocurrency communities fosters collaboration, knowledge sharing, and exposure to diverse perspectives. Engaging in discussions and asking questions contributes to continuous learning. Lastly, experimenting with different strategies, investment approaches, and risk management techniques helps individuals expand their skill set and gain practical experience.

Numerous resources are available to support continuous learning and skill development in the cryptocurrency market. Books and online courses offer in-depth knowledge on various cryptocurrency-related topics. Webinars and workshops conducted by industry professionals provide interactive learning experiences. Attending cryptocurrency conferences and events offers opportunities to learn from experts, network with peers, and gain exposure to the latest trends and developments. Online resources, such as cryptocurrency news websites, blogs, and reputable online publications, provide up-to-date information, market analysis, and educational content.

Developing a growth mindset is crucial for continuous learning and skill development. The idea that skills and intelligence can be developed through commitment and effort is what defines a growth mindset. In the cryptocurrency market, cultivating a growth mindset involves embracing challenges, seeking feedback, embracing failure, and maintaining persistence and discipline. Viewing challenges as opportunities for growth fosters resilience and an eagerness to overcome obstacles. Seeking feedback allows individuals to identify areas for improvement and refine their strategies. Embracing failure as a learning opportunity encourages resilience and adaptability. Persistence and discipline are necessary for establishing a regular learning schedule and embracing lifelong learning as a habit.

Applying continuous learning to the cryptocurrency market leads to numerous benefits and increases the chances of success. By staying updated with industry developments, adapting to market dynamics, and continuously enhancing knowledge and skills, individuals can improve trading and investment performance, navigate market uncertainty, build a strong professional network, and foster personal growth and fulfillment. Making educated decisions, adjusting to shifting market conditions, and contribute to the advancement of the industry are all made possible by continuous learning.

CHAPTER
X
Risk Warning and
Legal Considerations

Understanding the Risks of Cryptocurrency Trading

Cryptocurrency trading has gained significant popularity in recent years, attracting a growing number of traders and investors. However, it is crucial to understand and manage the risks associated with this dynamic market. High volatility, regulatory uncertainties, cybersecurity threats, and market manipulation characterize the cryptocurrency market. This section explores the risks involved in cryptocurrency trading, their potential impact, and strategies for managing and mitigating these risks to ensure informed decision-making and protect investments.

One of the primary risks of cryptocurrency trading is the high volatility and price fluctuations. Unlike traditional financial markets, cryptocurrency is known for its extreme price swings within short periods. The value of cryptocurrencies can skyrocket or plummet, leading to substantial gains or losses for traders and investors. The volatile nature of the market is influenced by factors such as market sentiment, regulatory developments, technological advancements, and global economic conditions. It is crucial for traders and investors to be prepared for the inherent volatility and to understand its potential impact on their investments.

Another significant risk in cryptocurrency trading is the regulatory and legal landscape. As the market for cryptocurrencies expands and gain attention from governments and regulatory bodies, there is ongoing uncertainty regarding the regulatory frameworks that will be applied. Different jurisdictions have varying regulations, and changes in regulations or government policies can significantly impact market sentiment, liquidity, and trading activities. Traders and investors must stay updated on regulatory developments and adhere to compliance requirements to mitigate regulatory risks.

The decentralized nature of cryptocurrencies introduces security and cybersecurity risks. Cryptocurrency exchanges and wallets can be attractive targets for hackers and cybercriminals seeking to exploit vulnerabilities. Hacking, theft, and fraud incidents have occurred, resulting in significant financial losses for individuals. Implementing robust security measures to protect investments and personal information is crucial. This includes using reputable exchanges with strong security protocols, utilizing hardware wallets for offline storage of cryptocurrencies, and practicing good cybersecurity hygiene such as regularly updating software, using strong passwords, and being cautious of phishing attempts.

Market manipulation is another significant risk in the cryptocurrency market. Cryptocurrencies are prone to numerous types of market manipulation because of their tiny size and lack of regulations. Practices such as pump-and-dump schemes, spoofing, and wash trading can artificially inflate or deflate prices, leading to misleading market signals. Traders must exercise caution and conduct thorough research to avoid falling victim to market manipulation. Relying on reputable sources of information, analyzing market trends and patterns, and being aware of suspicious activities can help mitigate the risk of market manipulation.

The ease with which a cryptocurrency can be purchased or sold without having a major impact on its price is referred to as liquidity risk. Some cryptocurrencies, especially those with lower market capitalization, may have lower liquidity, making it challenging to enter or exit positions quickly. Illiquid markets can result in slippage and increased trading costs. Traders and investors should consider liquidity risks when selecting cryptocurrencies and understand the potential impact on their trading strategies. It is important to evaluate the trading volume, depth of the order book, and the presence of market makers to assess liquidity conditions accurately.

Operational and technical risks are inherent in the cryptocurrency ecosystem. Exchange outages, technical glitches, and network congestion can impact trading activities and access to funds. Furthermore, human error, such as misplacing private keys or forgetting passwords, can lead to irreversible loss of funds. Selecting reputable exchanges with a track record of reliability, implementing proper security protocols, and maintaining backups of private keys are essential to minimize operational and technical risks. Staying updated with the latest security practices and technological advancements is crucial for mitigating such risks.

Managing and mitigating risks in cryptocurrency trading is crucial to protect investments and minimize potential losses. The following strategies can help traders and investors navigate the risks associated with this market:

Comprehensive research is essential before investing in any cryptocurrency. Understanding the project's fundamentals, team, partnerships, and potential market adoption can help assess its long-term viability and mitigate risks.

Diversification is a fundamental risk management strategy. Spreading investments across different cryptocurrencies, asset classes, and risk levels can reduce exposure to specific risks and minimize potential losses.

Defining risk tolerance levels and utilizing stop-loss orders can help manage downside risk. Stop-loss orders automatically trigger the sale of a cryptocurrency at a predetermined price, limiting potential losses if prices move against the trader's position.

Staying updated on regulatory developments and compliance requirements is crucial. Adhering to regulatory guidelines helps mitigate legal and regulatory risks associated with cryptocurrency trading.

Prioritize security by using reputable exchanges, employing hardware wallets, utilizing two-factor authentication, and practicing good cybersecurity hygiene. Regularly updating software, using strong passwords, and avoiding suspicious links or downloads are essential to protect investments.

Staying informed about market trends, news, and developments helps identify potential risks and opportunities. Being vigilant and cautious of market manipulation schemes is crucial. Relying on reputable sources for information and conducting thorough due diligence before making investment decisions is essential.

Regulatory Landscape and Legal Compliance

The cryptocurrency market has recently experienced tremendous growth and innovation, attracting global attention from investors, businesses, and regulators. As the market evolves, regulatory frameworks and legal compliance become crucial considerations for participants. This section explores the regulatory landscape surrounding cryptocurrencies and the importance of legal compliance in the industry. It delves into the challenges and opportunities regulations present, the impact on market participants, and strategies for navigating the complex regulatory environment.

The regulatory landscape for cryptocurrencies varies significantly across jurisdictions. Regulators worldwide are grappling with approaching this emerging asset class, balancing innovation with investor protection and systemic stability. Some countries have embraced cryptocurrencies, providing clear guidelines and regulatory frameworks, while others have expressed skepticism or implemented restrictive measures. The lack of global regulatory harmonization has created a complex and fragmented landscape that participants must navigate.

Regulatory efforts in the cryptocurrency market generally aim to achieve several objectives. These include consumer protection, prevention of money laundering and illicit activities, market integrity, financial stability, and investor confidence. However, regulators face several challenges when developing regulations for cryptocurrencies. These challenges include understanding the technology, keeping pace with market developments, addressing cross-border transactions, and striking a balance between innovation and risk management.

Regulations have a significant impact on various market participants in the cryptocurrency ecosystem. These include cryptocurrency exchanges, digital wallet providers, initial coin offering (ICO) projects, institutional investors, and individual traders. Regulatory requirements such as licensing, Know Your Customer (KYC) and Anti-Money Laundering (AML) procedures, reporting obligations, and tax compliance impose additional costs and operational burdens on businesses. Market participants must also consider the legal implications of their activities, including securities regulations, contract law, intellectual property rights, and consumer protection laws.

While navigating the regulatory landscape can be challenging, regulatory compliance offers several benefits to market participants.

Firstly, complying with regulations enhances investor protection by ensuring transparency, fairness, and accountability. It helps to weed out fraudulent schemes and bad actors, increasing trust in the market. Secondly, regulatory compliance attracts institutional investors who often require a robust legal framework and regulatory oversight. Their participation brings liquidity, stability, and mainstream adoption to the market. Lastly, complying with regulations can foster collaboration with traditional financial institutions, fostering innovation and integration between the traditional and cryptocurrency sectors.

Navigating the regulatory landscape requires a proactive and adaptive approach. Market participants can employ several strategies to ensure compliance and navigate the evolving regulatory environment effectively:

Stay updated on regulatory developments, guidelines, and legislation in relevant jurisdictions. Regularly monitor industry news, consult legal experts, and participate in industry conferences and working groups to stay ahead of regulatory changes.

Conduct thorough due diligence on the regulatory requirements of jurisdictions you operate or plan to engage in. Understand the specific compliance obligations, licensing requirements, and reporting obligations to ensure full compliance.

Establish internal compliance policies and procedures that adhere to regulatory requirements. Implement robust AML and KYC practices, adopt secure data management and privacy protocols, and maintain accurate and up-to-date records.

Actively engage with regulators, industry associations, and policymakers. Provide input, share expertise, and contribute to the development of regulatory frameworks. Building relationships and open lines of communication with regulators can foster a better understanding of the industry and influence regulatory decisions.

Collaborate with industry partners to share best practices, exchange knowledge, and collectively address regulatory challenges. Market participants can drive industry-wide compliance standards and promote self-regulatory initiatives by working together.

Advocate for clear and predictable regulatory frameworks. Engage in constructive dialogue with regulators, highlighting the benefits of balanced regulations that foster innovation while safeguarding market integrity and investor protection.

Embrace agility and flexibility to adapt to evolving regulations. Continuously monitor and assess the impact of regulatory changes on your business or investment strategies. Adjust compliance practices, operational processes, and risk management frameworks accordingly.

International cooperation plays a crucial role in shaping the regulatory landscape for cryptocurrencies. Collaboration among governments, regulatory bodies, and industry stakeholders is essential to foster harmonization, facilitate cross-border transactions, and establish consistent regulatory standards. Initiatives such as information sharing, regulatory sandboxes, and international agreements can promote coordination, knowledge exchange, and best practices across jurisdictions.

Tax Implications of Cryptocurrency Trading

Cryptocurrency trading has grown in popularity recently, drawing more participants eager to take advantage of the opportunities provided by digital assets. However, traders and investors must understand the tax implications associated with cryptocurrency trading. The tax landscape surrounding cryptocurrencies is intricate and varies across jurisdictions. This section explores the tax considerations and implications of cryptocurrency trading, including capital gains, income tax, reporting obligations, and strategies for navigating the complex tax landscape to ensure compliance and optimize tax outcomes.

Cryptocurrency trading involves various taxable events that can have significant tax implications. Identifying and understanding these events is crucial to ensure accurate tax reporting. The most common taxable events in cryptocurrency trading include capital gains or losses resulting from the sale or exchange of cryptocurrencies, income generated from mining activities, income received from staking, and the tax implications of airdrops and forks.

Capital gains tax is a critical consideration for cryptocurrency traders and investors. When cryptocurrencies are sold or exchanged for fiat currency or other digital assets, it typically triggers a capital gain or loss. The way capital gains are taxed is determined by the length of time that cryptocurrencies are held and by the local tax regulations.

When compared to long-term capital gains, short-term capital gains, which result from the sale of cryptocurrency held for a relatively short time, are typically subject to higher tax rates.

Income tax is another aspect of cryptocurrency trading that requires careful attention. Income derived from mining activities, which involve validating transactions and adding them to the blockchain, is generally considered taxable income. Additionally, income generated from staking, where cryptocurrencies are held within a blockchain network to support operations, may also be subject to income tax. The specific tax treatment of cryptocurrency-related income varies among jurisdictions and should be understood and complied with accordingly.

Cryptocurrency traders and investors are typically subject to reporting obligations to ensure proper tax compliance. Maintaining accurate records of cryptocurrency transactions, including purchase and sale dates, transaction values, and associated fees, is crucial for tax reporting purposes. Traders must report their cryptocurrency transactions and associated gains or losses on their tax returns, adhering to the specific reporting requirements of their jurisdiction. In some cases, foreign account reporting obligations may apply to cryptocurrency holdings in foreign exchanges, necessitating compliance with additional reporting requirements.

Traders and investors can employ various tax planning strategies to optimize tax outcomes and ensure compliance. These strategies include carefully selecting cost-basis identification methods, such as First-In-First-Out (FIFO) or Specific Identification, which can impact the calculation of capital gains and losses. Additionally, tax-loss harvesting can be used strategically to offset capital gains by selling cryptocurrencies at a loss. Exploring tax-advantaged accounts, such as Individual Retirement Accounts (IRAs) or Self-Invested Personal Pensions (SIPPs), can provide tax benefits for holding cryptocurrencies. Seeking professional advice from tax consultants or accountants experienced in cryptocurrency tax matters is highly recommended to ensure accurate tax reporting, compliance with regulations, and identification of tax planning opportunities.

The regulatory landscape surrounding cryptocurrency taxation is continuously evolving. Regulatory developments, such as guidance from tax authorities and legislative changes, can significantly impact tax obligations for cryptocurrency traders and investors. International cooperation and harmonization efforts among tax authorities play a crucial role in establishing consistent tax treatment and minimizing cross-border tax complexities. Staying informed about local tax laws, seeking professional advice, and actively monitoring regulatory developments are vital for traders and investors to navigate the ever-changing tax environment effectively.

Seeking Professional Advice

Cryptocurrency trading has emerged as a famous avenue for investors seeking to capitalize on the potential opportunities presented by digital assets. However, the complexities and risks of the cryptocurrency market require careful decision-making and a deep understanding of its intricacies. One of the most important strategies for overcoming the difficulties of cryptocurrency trading is to seek out professional advice from industry specialists. This section explores the importance of seeking professional advice, the areas where expertise is invaluable, the benefits of expert guidance, and strategies for finding and engaging with qualified professionals.

The cryptocurrency market operates on decentralized networks, distinct from traditional financial markets. Its valuation is influenced by various factors such as technological advancements, market sentiment, regulatory developments, and global economic conditions. Understanding these dynamics and their impact on trading decisions requires specialized knowledge of blockchain technology, market analysis, risk management, and legal and regulatory frameworks.

Expertise in technical analysis is crucial for evaluating market trends, chart patterns, and price movements. Professional traders possess the skills to identify potential entry and exit points, recognize support and resistance levels, and interpret indicators and oscillators effectively.

Professional advice provides insights into fundamental analysis, which involves assessing cryptocurrencies' underlying value and potential. Experts evaluate project fundamentals, including team experience, technology, market adoption, partnerships, and competition, enabling informed investment decisions.

Managing risk is paramount in cryptocurrency trading. Professionals can assist in setting risk tolerance levels, implementing stop-loss orders, and diversifying portfolios to minimize potential losses and protect investments.

The evolving regulatory landscape surrounding cryptocurrencies necessitates expert guidance to navigate tax implications, reporting obligations, and legal compliance. Professionals well-versed in cryptocurrency tax laws ensure accurate reporting and optimize tax outcomes.

Security is of utmost importance in the cryptocurrency market. Experts provide guidance on secure wallet management, best practices for protecting private keys, and navigating potential cybersecurity threats.

Professionals possess specialized knowledge acquired through years of experience and continuous learning. Their expertise allows them to interpret market trends, identify investment opportunities, and mitigate risks effectively.

Expert guidance helps traders and investors make well-informed decisions based on comprehensive analysis and risk assessment. Professionals provide objective insights, assisting individuals to avoid common pitfalls and make strategic trading choices.

The cryptocurrency market operates 24/7, and staying updated with market developments requires significant time and effort. Seeking professional advice allows traders and investors to leverage the expertise of professionals, saving time and energy while accessing valuable insights.

Professionals often have access to extensive networks and resources, including research tools, market data, and industry connections. This access enhances the quality and depth of analysis, providing traders and investors with a competitive edge.

As a result of the volatile nature of the cryptocurrency market, traders can make impulsive and irrational judgments. Professionals provide emotional support, helping individuals navigate market fluctuations and maintain a disciplined approach to trading.

Thorough research is essential to identify qualified professionals with expertise in specific areas of interest. Look for industry certifications, relevant experience, and positive client testimonials.

Seek recommendations from trusted sources, including fellow traders, investors, and industry associations. Referrals can provide valuable insights and help identify reputable professionals.

Schedule consultations or interviews with potential professionals to discuss their areas of expertise, approach to trading, and investment philosophy. This interaction helps gauge their knowledge, communication style, and compatibility with personal trading goals.

Establish open and continuous communication with the selected professional. Regularly share investment objectives, risk tolerance, and trading preferences to ensure a tailored approach to advice and support.

While relying on professional advice is valuable, it is crucial to continue learning and expanding one's knowledge in cryptocurrency trading. This allows traders and investors to better understand the advice received and make informed decisions based on their own assessments.

~ 151 ~

CONCLUSION

Recap of Key Points

Throughout this e-book, we have delved into various aspects of cryptocurrency trading, exploring market analysis, trading strategies, risk management, and the importance of professional advice. As we conclude our discussion, it is essential to recap the key points covered and reinforce the fundamental insights gained. This recap is a comprehensive review of the essential knowledge and principles for successful cryptocurrency trading.

I.   Understanding the Cryptocurrency Market

Digital assets known as cryptocurrencies use blockchain technology to operate on decentralized networks. They offer potential investment opportunities and are influenced by various factors such as technology advancements, market sentiment, and regulatory developments.

Successful trading requires a combination of technical and fundamental analysis. Technical analysis involves studying price charts, identifying trends, and using indicators to make trading decisions. Fundamental analysis evaluates cryptocurrencies' underlying value and potential by considering factors like team experience, technology, market adoption, partnerships, and competition.

II. Trading Strategies

Traders can choose between short-term and long-term strategies based on their trading goals and risk tolerance. Short-term trading focuses on exploiting short-term price fluctuations, while long-term trading involves holding positions for an extended period, capitalizing on the long-term growth potential of cryptocurrencies.

Day trading involves executing multiple trades within a single day to take advantage of intraday price movements. It requires close monitoring of the market and the use of technical analysis indicators to identify short-term trading opportunities.

Swing trading aims to capture shorter-term price swings within a larger trend. Based on price patterns and indicators, traders utilize technical analysis to identify trade entry and exit points.

Position trading involves holding positions for an extended period, often weeks or months, to take advantage of long-term market trends. Fundamental analysis plays a vital role in identifying promising cryptocurrencies for long-term investment.

III. Risk Management and Psychology

Understanding personal risk tolerance is crucial to avoid excessive exposure to market volatility. Traders must set risk tolerance levels and implement risk management strategies like stop-loss orders and portfolio diversification.

Emotions can negatively impact trading decisions. Developing emotional discipline, adhering to a trading plan, and using objective analysis can help traders make rational decisions and avoid impulsive actions driven by fear or greed.

IV. Professional Advice

Seeking guidance from professionals with specialized knowledge and experience in areas such as technical analysis, fundamental analysis, risk management, and tax compliance can provide valuable insights and support decision-making.

Researching, seeking referrals, and conducting consultations are effective strategies for finding and engaging with qualified professionals. Continuous communication and an ongoing learning mindset help foster a collaborative and productive relationship.

V. Regulatory and Legal Considerations

The regulatory environment surrounding cryptocurrencies is evolving. Traders and investors must stay informed about tax obligations, reporting requirements, and legal compliance in their respective jurisdictions.

Cryptocurrency trading can trigger tax obligations, including capital gains tax and income tax. Understanding tax laws, maintaining accurate records, and seeking professional advice can ensure compliance and optimize tax outcomes.

In this e-book, we have explored the fundamental aspects of cryptocurrency trading, covering market analysis, trading strategies, risk management, professional advice, and regulatory considerations. By understanding the basics of the cryptocurrency market, employing appropriate trading strategies, managing risk, seeking professional advice, and staying informed about regulatory requirements, traders can enhance their chances of success in this dynamic and evolving field. The recap of key points serves as a valuable reference, reinforcing the insights and knowledge necessary for informed decision-making and effective participation in cryptocurrency trading. With continuous learning, adaptability, and a disciplined approach, traders can navigate the complexities of the market and seize opportunities for profitable trading experiences.

Final Thoughts on Cryptocurrency Trading

Cryptocurrency trading has emerged as a transformative force, disrupting traditional finance and presenting a wealth of opportunities for investors and traders alike. Throughout this e-book, we have explored various aspects of cryptocurrency trading, including its rise and impact, opportunities and challenges, strategic approaches, risk management, emotional control, continuous learning, and the power of networking. As we conclude this comprehensive exploration, reflecting on the key insights gained and offering final thoughts on the exciting and ever-evolving world of cryptocurrency trading is crucial.

Cryptocurrencies have revolutionized the financial landscape, offering decentralized alternatives to traditional systems. With their potential for increased accessibility, financial inclusion, and wealth creation, cryptocurrencies have captured the imagination of individuals worldwide. Moreover, the underlying technology of cryptocurrencies, blockchain, has the power to reshape various industries beyond finance, creating a foundation for transparency, security, and efficiency.

Cryptocurrency trading presents a plethora of opportunities for financial growth. Rapid price movements, emerging technologies, and market inefficiencies offer traders and investors avenues for profit. However, the cryptocurrency market is also known for its volatility, regulatory uncertainties, and risks. Successfully navigating these challenges requires a strategic approach, disciplined risk management, and a deep understanding of market dynamics.

To excel in cryptocurrency trading, education and research are paramount. Staying informed about market trends, technological advancements, and regulatory changes enables traders to make informed decisions and adapt to the dynamic nature of the market. Developing a trading plan with clear objectives, risk tolerance levels, and entry and exit strategies provides a roadmap for success and minimizes emotional decision-making.

Effective risk management is essential for sustainable trading success. Setting risk parameters, such as establishing risk tolerance levels and implementing risk management strategies like stop-loss orders and portfolio diversification, protects capital and mitigates potential losses. Furthermore, the decentralized nature of cryptocurrencies requires heightened attention to security. Utilizing secure wallets, employing multi-factor authentication, and staying vigilant against phishing attempts are crucial steps to safeguarding assets.

Emotions play a significant role in trading decisions. Embracing emotional control and discipline allows traders to make rational choices based on analysis and strategy, rather than being swayed by fear or greed. By managing emotions and adhering to a well-defined trading plan, traders can avoid impulsive actions and stay focused on their long-term objectives.

Cryptocurrency trading is a rapidly evolving landscape that demands continuous learning and adaptation. Embracing lifelong learning, staying curious, and seeking out new information are essential for staying at the forefront of industry developments. Experimentation, adjusting strategies, and adopting new techniques enable traders to remain agile in the face of changing market conditions. Learning from mistakes and engaging with the community foster growth, innovation, and the expansion of professional connections.

Active participation in cryptocurrency communities, forums, and conferences fosters networking, collaboration, and exchanging ideas. Engaging with like-minded individuals, sharing insights and experiences, and seeking professional advice accelerates learning and improves trading outcomes. Experienced professionals offer specialized knowledge, industry connections, and mentorship that can guide traders towards success.

As we conclude our exploration of cryptocurrency trading, it is clear that this dynamic and transformative field holds immense potential for financial growth, innovation, and personal development. By approaching cryptocurrency trading with a strategic mindset, managing risks effectively, maintaining emotional control, engaging in continuous learning, and leveraging the power of networking, traders can confidently navigate the complexities of the market and seize opportunities in the digital asset space. Cryptocurrency trading is an exciting frontier that demands dedication, perseverance, and a commitment to ongoing education. By embracing the ever-evolving nature of the market, staying adaptable, and harnessing the power of knowledge and collaboration, traders can thrive and contribute to the advancement of this groundbreaking industry. With each trade, each interaction, and each learning opportunity, traders embark on a journey of growth and exploration, shaping their own path in the captivating world of cryptocurrency trading.

Thank you for buying and reading/listening to our book.
If you found this book useful/helpful please take a few minutes and
leave a review on the platform where you purchased our book.
Your feedback matters greatly to us.